# *the* **Bankruptcy of Academic Policy**

AN ORIGINAL PROMETHEUS PAPERBACK

# The Bankruptcy of Academic Policy

**PETER CAWS**

**S. DILLON RIPLEY**

**PHILIP C. RITTERBUSH**
(editor)

 Published by **Acropolis Books Ltd.**, Washington, D.C. 20009

## THE PROMETHEUS SERIES OF ORIGINAL PAPERBACKS

### THE BANKRUPTCY OF ACADEMIC POLICY
Peter Caws, S. Dillon Ripley, Philip C. Ritterbush

### RESEARCH INSTITUTIONS OF THE FUTURE
AAAS Symposium, December, 1971

### TALENT WASTE
Institutional Malfunction in the Market for Skilled Manpower

### THE LEARNING MACHINE
The Impact of Communications Technology on Higher Education and Research

**ACROPOLIS BOOKS**
*Colortone Building, 2400 17th St., N.W.*
*Washington, D.C. 20009*

*Printed in the United States of America by*
**COLORTONE PRESS, Creative Graphics Inc.**
*Washington, D.C. 20009*

**Library of Congress Catalog Number 72-75040**
Standard Book Number 87491-500-7

# Contents

January, 1972                    Volume One, number three

Peter Caws — The Goals and Governance of Universities Regarded as Institutions of Learning — 7

S. Dillon Ripley — Truth and Institutions; Reflections on the 125th Anniversary of the Smithsonian Institution — 35

Philip C. Ritterbush — Regaining the Policy Initiative in the Modern University — 41

COLLOQUIUM: Extending the Foundations of Academic Policy

Thomas H. Maher — Proposal: The Promotion of Learning as the Central Objective of the University — 63

Review Essay — Subordinating Management to Policy: George S. Odiorne, *Management Decision by Objectives*(1969) — 65

Robert S. McMeekin — Alternative Approaches to Planning and Policy in Higher Education — 70

Donald P. Jacobs
Almarin Phillips — Knowledge of Financial Institutions as the Basis for National Policy on Financial Structure and Regulation — 74

Michael Marien — Proposal: A Census of Education and Learning — 77

Norman P. Uhl            Identifying Institutional Goals      83

Allen P. Splete          The Role of the Academic
                         Planning Officer in Innovation      92

Davis, Brody &           User Requirements: Analytic
Associates               Techniques for Academic
                         Architecture                        97

Digest of Literature                                         114

Other Literature Cited                                       124

Index                                                        126

## ILLUSTRATIONS

Prometheus                        After Hans Erni by
Stage design for the play            Ralph Logan
by Aeschylus (1947)

The Science Complex               Davis, Brody & Associates
State University of New York
at Binghamton

  Overall Site Plan                                    Cover
  Problem Structure Diagram                            99
  Elevations                                           108-111
  Scoring Grid Diagrams                                112-13

University of York                Valerie Thornton            34
                                  (by permission, Times
                                  Newspapers, Ltd.)

British University                H.M. Post Office            40,62,96
Architecture

Model for Problem-Solving and     G.S. Odiorne                66
Decision-Making by Objectives

Taxonomy of the Core Curriculum,  Igor Ansoff                 69
Vanderbilt Graduate School of
Management

Profile of Institutional Goals    Norman P. Uhl               99

# The Goals and Governance of Universities Regarded as Institutions of Learning

Peter Caws
Professor of Philosophy
Hunter College, City University of New York

> The end of anything would be that which could not be accomplished, or not so well accomplished, by any other thing.
>
> Plato, *Republic* 353

The following essay was written for and stimulated by the Assembly on University Goals and Governance. Its title borrows from that of the Assembly and also reflects a limitation of the Assembly's interest. The borrowing preserves an ordering of the concepts of "goals" and "governance": goals are taken to *precede* governance, in the sense that rational discussion of the governance of universities is considered futile in the absence of a clear specification of their goals. Implicit in this ordering is a certain view of the kind of social organization the university is.

For an organization to have goals at all it must be such as either (1) to seek its own ends or (2) to seek the ends of some other entity for which it is responsible or to which it is accountable or both. Case (1) gives an autonomous institution, case (2) not, unless the goals of the other entity (a community, a state, a tradition) are freely assumed as its own. In the case of the university it seems clear that the ends served are not those of the institution in itself but are always at least claimed to be the ends of society, or of a scholarly tradition, etc. And it is not clear that the university could even in principle serve other ends and remain a university. So that while one might insist on a form of practical autonomy on the grounds that no *other* body or institution or organization could know *better* the ends that the university ought to serve, still those ends cannot be arbitrary and the university must be (as indeed it generally has been) *answerable* in some way, to some critic or judge of its activities, for the nature and quality of those activities. This critic and judge is often referred to as a "constituency"; one of the important unresolved questions is just what constitutes this constituency.

This conclusion is important for a consideration of governance because it makes clear the fact that the university is not a fortuitous association of free agents, but a deliberate association of responsible agents. The forms of government appropriate to the two cases are quite different. In a fortuitous association of free agents—a town, a state, a nation—common goals emerge from the process of governance, beginning (let us assume) from democratic assumptions of equality. Democratic assumptions operate when there is no *a priori* reason to suppose that private persons should behave in one way rather than another—when there is no Divine voice, speaking directly or mediated by a king, and no transcendent historical necessity, perceived directly or mediated by a party. In a deliberate association of responsible agents, on the other hand, the nature of the responsibility does prescribe certain forms of behavior—provided at least that it is understood—and the deliberate character of the association means that persons are in some sense no longer private but already committed to common ends. This distinction is enough to show that a simple application of democratic theory to the university is not appropriate. It might be appropriate if the university were autonomous in the strong sense, but even then only at times when the nature of the ends or the responsibilities had become unclear.

Let us assume for purposes of argument that the ends the university serves are the ends, however determined, of the society and/or culture to which it belongs. (According to the interpretation of the "and/or" rather different conceptions of the university might emerge.) It can claim practical autonomy, according to the analysis given above, on condition that it genuinely makes those ends its own, and this is possible only on condition that the ends are sought out, clarified, justified and so on. Does the university as we know it *in fact* serve the ends of its society and/or culture? or are some or all of its ends not perhaps ends which are not in any sense those of its society or culture?

To pose the question in this way will already be seen by radicals as a capitulation to the *status quo;* the university does indeed serve its society only too well, they argue, and it must therefore be destroyed, as in the title of a recent article by Andre Gor, "Destroy the University" (21022) (April, 1970), *Partisan Review,* Vol. 38 (1971), pp. 314-318. But this assumes that the society wants to be what it is, that its only end is its own preservation as it is. It is not incompatible with the view of the university as the servant of its society to say that it should be the critic and the conscience of its society; to be an adversary is also, under appropriate circumstances, to be a defender, as the form of the parliamentary and judicial system makes clear. The adversary relation can however be conceived under two different modes: as the loyal opposition, devoted to improving the state of affairs by correcting policy, in pursuit perhaps of ends the society has forgotten or doesn't yet know it has, but which are nevertheless its true ends; or as the revolutionary force, devoted to combating and overthrowing the *status quo* and all it consciously or unconsciously desires or stands for.

The difficulty with the second of these modes has always been that the revolutionaries, in spite of themselves, in fact *embody* the main features of the *status quo;* they have been reared in it and have absorbed it, and their rejection of it is never more than partial, being as a rule the rejection only of some glaring but superficial elements of it. In consequence they carry through to the post-revolutionary regime most of the characteristics they claim to abhor, so that no revolution, however total it seemed at the time, has really succeeded in changing the deep structure of any society (which is not incidentally to be confused with its economic base). To abandon the strategy of violent revolution does not mean to abandon the eventual hope that society might become what the revolution, if successful, would have made it; nor does it mean settling for *mere* reform, if what is meant by this is that the essential quality of the society remains unchanged. It is curious that a movement which claims dialectics as its philosophical basis should have missed the point of the law according to which quantitative change can become qualitative change: it follows from that law that the accumulation of reform might indeed *be* the true revolution. And in another respect also the rhetoric of revolution has hindered rather than helped the correction of deficiencies, since it has served to discredit—by association with violence and repression—an analysis of social institutions that in the absence of these associations might well be accepted as plausible. I refer to the Marxist theory of the state, whose application to the university I shall develop further below.

At all events, for the purposes at hand I inscribe the university in its society. There are two main ways in which it might make a mistake about its goals: it might serve ends which are not in fact those of its society, or it might serve ends which genuinely are the ends of its society but which are in fact already better served by other institutions. I think that the university as presently constituted habitually makes both of these mistakes; in their most obvious forms they consist, under the first heading, of trying to provide *universal* higher education, and under the second of trying to provide at the same time certain forms of elementary *training*. But to show that these activities are mistakes requires two things: on the one hand a convincing argument that they are unnecessary or being more successfully carried on by other social institutions, and on the other a plausible account of what activities the university ought to be pursuing, if not these. And this requires in turn some comment on the society itself and on its institutions, as well as on the university.

The *raison d'être* of all the institutions of a democratic society is the service of the people. In Lincoln's formula "for the people" is the phrase most easily overlooked, partly again because of more recent associations—people's parties, people's governments, power to the people, all expressions which for good or bad reasons make Lincoln's heirs uneasy. *Of* the people, surely; *by* the people, because of elections and because anybody, in principle, can aspire to be President or at any rate a minor civil servant. But *for* the people: that, in the light of some recent actions of government, is not so clear. But I intend to insist upon it at least for government of the university. In so far as the university is an institution of its society, its responsibility is to ask itself how it can best serve the people. But that does not necessarily mean letting them all in, nor going out and offering them things.

By way of analogy, let us consider another institution, one which as far as I know had its origin in America (as indeed the public-service university did)—I mean the National Park. The park encloses a natural resource (plant and animal populations, geological formations and the like) and protects it against various forms of exploitation; it serves, in human terms, two distinct classes of people, on the one hand visitors who come to it in order to enjoy what it protects, to widen their experience, etc., and on the other hand naturalists who come to study what it protects, to add to our knowledge of it, in short to do research. Its personnel similarly consists of two classes, on the one hand those who guide the visitors and minister to their well-being and curiosity, and on the other those whose task it is to conserve the resource on which the naturalists work. The analogy to the university hardly needs spelling out: the resource is, briefly put, knowledge in its various developed and living forms, together with a certain set of attitudes and competences with respect to it; this knowledge is to be protected against the degradation of popular culture, military and political exploitation, and commercial gain. Students come to acquaint themselves with knowledge as *embodied* in their teachers (otherwise they could stay home and read books) and in some cases to study it in depth and even make contributions to it; scholars, in their turn, come to cultivate and enlarge it. Teachers play a guiding role; scholars again, as well as librarians and laboratory workers, etc., play a conserving one.

The principle of the admission of visitors to parks is that nobody who presents himself for entrance is turned away, and nobody who does not actually despoil what they contain (whether or not he profits from it) is ejected. Not everybody goes to parks; it has not become a widespread belief that people who go there make more money than people who don't (although that is probably the case statistically, if only because the under-privileged can't afford to go there at all) and the parks have not had an announced policy of limiting the number of visitors, although some of them are apparently working towards this simply because the natural resource cannot survive the human onslaught to which it has recently been subjected. The organization of the park as a park serves three constituencies, if I may so put it: the natural resource itself, the visitors, and the naturalists. It does not serve the guides and conservators, rather they serve the others—a point whose analogical implications for the teaching faculty need to be weighed when questions of governance are discussed. If trouble arises, there is no doubt as to the relative priorities of these constituencies: the first responsibility of the park is to the natural resource it protects, its next responsibility to the naturalists, and its last responsibility to the visitors. When the cave-paintings at Lascaux began to deteriorate the public was excluded, and everybody at once saw the justice of this. The natural resource comes first because it is considered to be as it were in trust for future generations of naturalists and visitors even if intermediate generations must be denied access to it. And the naturalists come next because their work is a precondition for the visitors' intelligent enjoyment of the park, on two counts: the knowledge they acquire about the natural resource is indispensable to its conservation, and their acquaintance with it provides the basis for selective (although not compulsory) attention on the part of the visitors. Again the analogy is obvious: the university's first responsibility is to the intellectual heritage, to use a banal but accurate expression, it receives in trust from earlier generations and holds in trust for future ones, its next responsibility is to the research faculty (not, I repeat, the teaching faculty), and its third responsibility is to the students who happen at any moment to be passing through it.

This ordering is not intended to belittle the importance of students; indeed collectively and over time it is precisely through the students that the university interacts with its society. But if a group of visitors to a national park were to insist that some unique feature of it be destroyed or despoiled for their convenience or gratification, on the grounds that the park existed in the long run for the benefit of its visitors, we would all see at once the distinction between the class of all visitors past, present, and future on the one hand, and the contingent subclass of visitors who happened at that moment to be there on the other. The implication of this contrast is that students who participate in university government need to think of themselves as representatives not only of their contemporaries but also of their class in a more general sense. And of course once this is said it is clear that the faculty and administrators too, while their association with the university is on the average longer than the average student's, need to be able to transcend the present and immediate in their consideration of policy. They seem usually to be able to do this quite well, so well in fact that they sometimes ignore the present and immediate altogether, which is not the intention of the term "transcend." But all too often under the aspect of eternity lurks the reality of short-range self-interest.

There are other reasons why everybody does not go to national parks: that kind of thing is boring to people of certain temperaments, it takes a certain effort to get there, there are plenty of other ways of spending time and money, plenty of other places where nature is accessible to the observer but where perhaps also the amenities of civilization are better developed, and so on. Parks are the natural environment for naturalists, but they may be far from the usual circuit of the visitor, and life in them may involve him in unaccustomed austerity. Something of the same kind could be said for the university. And yet for some reason increasing numbers of people want to go *there*. The question arises as to what they expect to get out of it and whether their expectation is justified, but the prior question is how that expectation was generated, why, in other words, there should be such a population pressure on the university system.

It is necessary at this point to make a crucial distinction which has not been clearly made. I said earlier that nobody who takes the trouble to make the trip and to present himself for admission to a National Park is excluded (unless some overriding consideration comes into play, as in the case of Lascaux). If however word were to get about that some group in the society, say an underprivileged minority, was because of some perhaps innocent-looking or unintentionally discriminatory regulation system-atically excluded from them, one might expect large numbers of these people to descend on the entrances in order to challenge this practice, even though they might have little genuine interest in what was to be found inside. They would be perfectly justified in doing this (and once inside, for that matter, might find the place interesting after all). If in this way everybody made a point of going to the parks, their resources would soon be destroyed. The distinction to be made is between *excluding nobody* and *including everybody*. If I know that I have free access to something, I will take advantage of it or not according to my true interests; but if I feel that my freedom of access is threatened, I may insist on taking advantage of it just to counteract that threat. (When landowners have tried to close rights of way large numbers of citizens have been known to walk over them even though they had no interest in going where they led.) I believe that in some cases (not all) the pressure on university admissions on the part of the minorities springs from something like this, although with a twist, namely that while many of those walking the right of way have no interest in going where it *really* leads, they believe because of all the other people crowding along it that there must be something to be gained by going there. The truth of the matter is that most of the others have no true interest in it either, but are similarly misled by false representations as to the beatitude that awaits the lucky fellow who completes the course, and urged on by shouts of encouragement from their elders.

Nobody perhaps really means to hold out a chimera before aspirants to the higher learning; but in all honesty, what *are* its benefits to the majority of the population who occupy the middle ranges of the Gaussian distribution of intelligence? (I do *not* mean here those who come out with an average I.Q. score on present tests, the discriminatory character of which may very well be demonstrable in the light of more equitable concepts of intelligence, considering cultural and linguistic variables, etc. I do however assume that talent of whatever sort, and aptitude for various kinds of activity—among which university studies are only one kind, and by no means necessarily the most honorable—are distributed normally in the population.) University studies have been assumed, first, to confer economic advantages; the average compensation for university-trained people is higher than for non-university-trained. What this bare fact does not reveal is that within categories occupied by both university-trained and non-university-trained personnel—and this includes most middle-level sales and management positions as well as a great number of positions in industry and the service professions—there is no detectable financial advantage to having been to the university; as Andrew Carnegie pointed out in 1885, the only difference that going to the university makes is a loss of four years' seniority in the business. The financial edge is felt only in professions occupied *exclusively* by university-trained persons; and only a small percentage of those who enter the university can get into these, a percentage that will in fact drop rather than remaining steady as the enrollment in universities grows. As far as that goes, there is no sound reason why even members of the most lucrative professions—law and medicine—should *have* to have been to the university; it is a tradition of this society that they should, but other societies have found other solutions, such as entering medical school directly from high school, becoming articled to a lawyer (a kind of apprenticeship), etc.

The second kind of advantage that university studies are considered to confer is cultural; the student is put in touch with the intellectual and artistic heritage of his society, and so on. But this is surely a reflection of a grave maladjustment in society; the nation's intellectual and artistic heritage and its cultural advantages ought to be distributed through it and available to all its members, and if the form of this distribution is in fact the distribution of universities throughout the society, then access to these general public goods ought not to depend on people's enrolling as students in them. Universities clearly do play a cultural role with respect to the communities in which they are located; other institutions (the church, the school, the library, the dramatic society etc.) play this role in communities that have no university. But for its students, the university must do much more than merely provide access to the various forms of culture. It does do this, of course, and in an especially concentrated form—my point is that if this is *all* it does, then it is, first, a remedial institution, since this range ought to be provided in the schools and in society at large, and second, a discriminatory institution, since whatever pieties we may subscribe to it is quite clear that higher education will never be *truly* universal and the remedy will therefore not be available to all. (The true remedy is to take the cultural resources to the people, a task for which the equipment is finally available, although it is as yet used very timidly. One encouraging move in this direction is the National Humanities Series, administered by the Woodrow Wilson Foundation for the National Endowment for the Humanities.)

A third claim, less frequent now perhaps than a generation or so ago, is that the universities contribute to the goal of the educational process in general that goes by the title of "preparation for citizenship." Of course this *is* the goal of the educational system in so far as it *is* universal; the reason why a democracy requires public education is not that it wishes to confer advantages on its citizens but that it cannot have citizens nor be a democracy if everybody is not educated. But this education must be *truly* universal and it must be compulsory for all who are going to be voters, and this means that it must be *finished* within the period of compulsory education and before the voting age. The consequences for public education of the recent lowering of the voting age are in fact much greater than anybody seems to have realized; among other things the change removes the last claim of the colleges to have anything to do with universal education in so far as the necessity for this follows from a democratic form of government. But then it has been one of the weaknesses of the American republic that it has almost never made the connection between public education and its form of government.

There was to be sure a great "education for citizenship" movement in professional education some years back, but it made the mistake of thinking that there was an intellectual discipline called "citizenship" the contents of which could be taught like physics and mathematics, whereas in fact of course the requirements for citizenship are precisely knowing enough physics and mathematics (and history and philosophy and literature, etc.) to enable any individual to make the decisions and choices necessary in the exercise of his duties as a citizen, which include not only voting at various levels but also following the actions of the government and making it aware of any dissatisfaction at the content of its policies or the manner of carrying them out, and in general *behaving* in such a way, not only with respect to the government but also with respect to fellow citizens, as to make the smooth functioning of the society possible.

The basic issue in public education comes down to the question of what a state can *require* of its people, and this can be only the minimum necessary to ensure that the institutions of the state and the freedom of its citizens are preserved. The educational system of a democracy should have as its highest ambition to make the children entrusted to it into free moral agents and then turn them loose. What makes this task challenging is that *an ignorant man cannot be free.* And the time allowed for the achieving this result is determined, as remarked above, by the society's convention as to the age of maturity, which on very many grounds is now fixed in our society at eighteen. Three things follow from this: first, if the schools cannot perform the task, then a democratic society is impossible; second, if they could but do not then a democratic society has not yet been achieved; third, if for either of these reasons education necessary for citizenship is put off until after eighteen (i.e. put into the universities) then as long as one single person of whatever intelligence does not go to the university, higher education is discriminatory.

The charge of discrimination would again have to be made if the business of the university were to prove to be motivation for learning, integration with peer groups, interpersonal relations, the search for identity, and the like, as so many people are beginning to claim it is. For again, *all* members of the society need these things, and there is *no* ground on which, for such objectives, admission to the university could be justified for some and not others. In fact, unless one is prepared to accept a purely economic determination of privilege (surely an untenable position by now) one is forced to choose between indiscriminate admission to the university on the one hand, and recognition on the other of a function which it, and no other institution, is uniquely capable of fulfilling, and from which some, and not all, of the members of the population are capable of profiting. If the university allows itself to be persuaded that its mission, or any part of it, is a kind of general socialization, the self-realization of its students, the therapeutic relief of those crises of adolescence that the structure and behavior of our society have done so much to exacerbate, then it really will destroy itself. Not that it cannot or even ought not to do these things, but they can only be incidental to its true business. They cannot be the things it sets out to do but at most something ancillary that it finds necessary to do in order to facilitate its proper function.

That function, as I have already assumed, has to do with knowledge, its conservation, extension, and dissemination, and the defense and communication of certain attitudes towards it. No neat formula, of course, will suffice; but the fact that it is assumed without question that two of the primary activites that go on in the university are learning and teaching confirms this association with knowledge. (Remember that knowledge is not only *knowing that* but also *knowing how*—and there can be other variants on this formula; I shall simply assume that anything that can be learned is a form of knowledge.) Such a specification of the function of the university seems archaic to some people who for one reason or another wish not to be constrained by a primary allegiance to knowledge, because other things seem more urgent or more relevant, but the delusion involved in this is that of supposing that institutions with given structures can change their functions at will. There are, to be sure, some parts of universities—more so in some institutions than in others—adapted for these secondary ends: dormitories, counseling services, and the like; but without the intellectual center these would just become communes and quasi-psychiatric clinics, which might very well exist independently of the university.

In fact, although it is a commonplace to say that the university must now take over the functions of the family, because the family is declining and the university seems the only place, apart from the schools (where the same thing goes on at an earlier stage) in which late adolescents can find any personal identification at all, it might be worth giving some thought to the possibility of reinstituting the family under a different form, rather than loading the moral and sentimental education of the young on to an institution which is already charged with their intellectual education. The hippie movement should be given credit for trying, outside the university and on the basis of a totally different kind of alliance, to do something of this sort. Similarly for the churches, which might, freed of their dogmatic and liturgical baggage, still find a role to play in a modern society. Television has more or less successfully taken over a large part of the function of entertainment formerly provided by circuses, road companies, and amateur theatricals, and similar metamorphoses in other areas of life seem not implausible.

And in any case, all this contrived talk of self-realization, the education of affect, and the like, is extraordinarily patronizing. The university has been criticized on the grounds of its irrelevance, but as far as I know it has rarely been asked to take in hand these extra-intellectual tasks as a specific charge. The students may say that the courses are dull and impersonal, and they may think that it would be better if they were dull and personal; but my conviction is that everybody would be better satisfied if, in spite of remaining impersonal, the courses became interesting. If we really took care of the intellectual appetites of our students, with all the variations in those appetites induced by current events, we would not have to contort ourselves into clumsy therapeutics. The way to begin this is to find out what the students' intellectual appetites are. It may turn out that some of them genuinely don't have any, are as it were tone-deaf intellectually; it would be more honest, in that case, to point out that they can probably get what they want better elsewhere. It may be, again, that the intellectual appetites of some of them are narrowly channeled, and are directed towards well-defined career goals. In that case it might be more honest to direct them to those training centers where the appropriate pedagogy for that particular objective has been worked out.

Such training centers, of course, already exist; they belong, however, not to the universities but to the civil service, the airlines, the unions, and so on. It is not the case that organizations like this direct their attention only to the special techniques of their own trade—the training curricula include many subjects, such as mathematics, English, even social studies, normally covered in the liberal arts curriculum. And it is remarkable how efficiently teachers of these subjects, when they are part of a training program for professionals, go about their business. They would simply not think of putting a student in a classroom for three hours a week, fifteen weeks a semester, five semesters running, in order to make him proficient in a foreign language. Nor would they engage in laborious experiments to find a better mix; they would simply count on the motivation, and put the material forward as rapidly as possible and organized in the best way found empirically, *in that situation,* to lead to the surest results. Unless it wishes to turn itself into a kind of training institution, a task for which it is poorly fitted because of the organization of its calendar and teaching schedule, it is pointless for the university to try this. The most obvious difficulty lies with faculty teaching loads: no faculty member operating at nine contact hours a week could possible make more than a marginal contribution to such a training program, and it is in fact outrageous that anybody should be paid at faculty rates for doing nine hours of *that* kind of work each week. The nine hour teaching load is linked to independent work, just as the summer vacation is, and the sabbatical. Berlitz instructors do not get almost a third of the year as paid vaction, and they do not earn sabbaticals. Only if some internal distinction among faculty members were to be introduced, so that some of them would go back to twenty and twenty-five hour teaching schedules, could this efficient pedagogy of training be incorporated into the university. And yet in fact almost all the elementary courses taught in liberal arts colleges are precisely of this sort. The country is wasting millions of dollars on them annually.

One notable feature of some of the most successful professional training programs is a complete lack of any hierarchical relationship between teacher and student. One would ordinarily expect that a man teaching airline pilots complicated techniques of flying and navigation would have to be somebody with a good deal of flying experience, which would confer upon what he said an appropriate authority. But in fact the people responsible for setting up these training programs are not in the least concerned with the question whether the teacher has flying experience or not, provided he can follow the lecture outline which has been prepared. The only reason they use him is that he is cheaper than a machine. His presence does, of course, make the situation more human, but that is merely an incidental advantage. The heart of the matter lies in the fact that failure to learn the techniques correctly, at least in this special case, may have rather drastic consequences. One cannot perhaps expect, for training ancillary to university studies, motivations in terms of life and death, but one can surely expect some motivation other than the authority of the teacher. As a matter of fact, the widespread use of graduate assistants, hardly older than the students themselves, for elementary courses constitutes a tacit recognition of the remedial or training character of these courses; what is rarely confronted is the *prima facie* absurdity of having senior faculty also teach such courses (if graduate students can do it) or conversely of consigning them to graduate students (if senior faculty are needed). The absurdity would be reduced if *some* senior faculty—those who like that sort of thing, are good at it, and don't particularly want, or have the talent, to do research—were designated as university teachers (rather than professors) and given suitable titles and class loads. They could elect to go, along with the graduate assistants and all the elementary and survey courses in all subjects, into a University Teaching Institute linked administratively to the university proper, where the student would spend as much time as was necessary to acquire the background and training he needed for his university studies. Faculty members would be given an option between heavy teaching loads in the Institute, compensated by early tenure (to be broken only by incompetence), no pressure of publication, escalator-type promotion at fixed intervals, etc., and light teaching loads in the university proper, balanced by delayed (or no) tenure, serious research expectations, promotion on merit, etc. If there were a provision for transfer under suitable circumstances from one sequence to the other, and due attention to the semantics of the situation (so that teachers would not feel inferior to professors—maybe they should be called "Doctors," for example) the universities might find that they would get a lot more good teaching, and a lot less bad research, out of their present faculties.

The student in the Institute would learn what the teachers in it were teaching: at this level the symmetry between teaching and learning can still be considered to hold. Something happens to this symmetry, however, at the university level; it is notable that while the expression "higher learning" has a current use and recognized meaning, no parallel expression "higher teaching" has entered the language. I take the university to be, precisely, an institution of higher learning—a place where the student goes when he has exhausted the resources of the *teaching* institutions available to him (the high schools, the Institutes, the trade and professional schools) but wishes to cultivate his learning still further. For this he needs an environment provided with tools and examples, and these the university and its faculty can provide. What it and they cannot provide is the motivation, the intellectual appetite that causes learning to take place in situations where explicit teaching is no longer feasible. They can discover or stimulate these appetites but they cannot create them.

University studies proper begin, therefore, at the point where it is reasonable to raise the question whether what is to be learned can be taught or not. This will easily be recognized as a reference to Plato, which, since his Academy was the first university, is not inappropriate. In one sense, therefore, "pedagogy" has no place in the university; the etymological origins of the work link it explicitly, first (from *pais, paidos,* a child, heir, descendant) to the business of bringing up the new generation, which as we have seen must be essentially finished before university entrance if the age of 18 is to mark the threshold of adulthood—a point I may seem to be stressing unduly but whose importance is cardinal—and second (from *ago,* I lead, *agogos,* a leader, guide) to a controlled or planned process, a teaching process, in fact. But in higher education it is far more important to work a change in the student's understanding of the potential for learning offered by his intersection with the university, than to make any adjustment in patterns of teaching. Learning, as Saul Touster has pointed out, goes on in all the curricula, plain, extra- and meta-, but it might go on better still without any "curriculum" at all, since that inevitably suggests a course to be run which is somehow set out in advance. The best learning is a kind of exploration, not one contrived by somebody else but one which springs from the student's own sense of possibility and wonder. Strictly speaking, we can't teach him anything, and he will truly learn only what his inner conviction suggests to him is worth the effort. It is because of the failure to encourage such motivation that such a disquieting proportion of what goes on in universities is a waste of time. This approach, it is true, puts a burden on the student to take himself in hand, but he need not be left entirely alone while he makes the decision what to do. The practical arrangements for genuinely *higher* learning I will come to in a minute; before that it may be worth while to point out some respects in which it is frustrated in the present system. The chief source of frustration is a sort of conspiracy to prevent the student from imagining that it is even possible to take himself in hand at all in a university setting. The elements of this conspiracy are placement tests, basic requirements, grades, and degrees.

At entry to the university, the student is evaluated. Some kind of evaluation probably determined whether he was admitted at all, and he is likely to take a series of placement tests designed to put him in this level or that of mathematics or foreign languages. This evaluation is a ˙sorting device (as indeed the earlier one was too); it tells the administration where to put the student, it tells the student nothing. But the student, when he enters the university, is a full grown, autonomous adult human being. What business has the university to put him anywhere, or to demand anything of him? What it ought to do is to ask him why he came and what he wants to do; and an uncertain response to either of these questions should be met by an explanation of what the university does and a demonstration of what might happen to him if he committed himself to various different courses of study, which ought to be laid out so that he can see what they involve and where they eventually lead. As it is, people pour into the universities without ever being asked whether or why they want to go there and embark on courses of study which are either completely determined (the basic requirements) or completely undetermined (the electives); advice, if it is given at all, is given by people who know very little about the institution as a whole—specialists either in one of its departments or, what is worse, in a generalized kind of counseling. The only person who is really in a position to tell the student what the university can offer is somebody who really knows what it can offer, and this is not in terms of formal requirements and degrees, but in terms of intellectual content. Such people are almost non-existent; they ought to be trained. Their training would build on first-order or direct knowledge in one area (knowledge that involves command of the field and readiness to engage without preparation in technical discussions of substantial issues in it) and would extend to the other departments of the university by way of second-order or indirect knowledge (knowledge that involves acquaintance with the field and ability to engage in intelligent discussions of issues in it after the consultation of standard works of reference and other sources) and paradigmatic knowledge (knowledge that comes from some exemplary experience with a problem in the field, confronted under the guidance of an expert in it). And they would then be equipped to act as consultants to new—or for that matter to advanced—students, to offer seminars or courses that would orient students to the resources of the university and their intellectual distribution (the "map of knowledge," as it has sometimes been called).

What the students did with this information would depend, as is usual with maps. on where they wanted to go. The principle that they ought to know something about the scope of available human wisdom is acknowledged in many universities by the familiar "basic requirements" or "distribution requirements," which involve as a rule a sampling of unrelated courses in disparate fields. A degree of compulsion is involved in this even when an apparently generous selection of alternatives is offered. (The greater the selection, of course, the less plausible the requirement.) The grotesque inappropriateness of this system can hardly be overstressed: the student does get exposed to *some* variety of subject-matter, it is true, but learning little bits of this and that, whether arbitrarily or randomly, does not lay a serious foundation for anything. It would be better to adapt the principle of second-order or indirect knowledge, outlined above, and insist that the student know *about* the whole range of available knowledge, even that he have paradigmatic experiences of the various fields (which does not mean mastering some body of principles but rather engaging, under supervision, in some representative inquiry or argument), but that he acquire first-order or direct knowledge only in some limited areas which his acquaintance with the map suggests to him may be of interest.

In these areas—but in no others—his work would need to be graded. The present scheme of attaching grades to work at all stages of the student's career and in all areas, and computing these into a cumulative average, is, of all the insane practices now to be encountered in the university, the most incredibly lunatic. Phrenological testing or the casting of horoscopes are coldly rational by comparison with it. It pretends to condense the complexity of an entire university career into a decimal number between 0 and 4 or some equivalent letter. Larger numbers are bad enough—College Board scores, Graduate Record Examinations, percentiles and so on—but the Cumulative Grade Point Average remains as the prize living monument to bureaucratic efficiency and academic mindlessness. The only *sensible* thing I have ever heard of anyone's doing even with the A.B.C. system of grading was done at Bucknell University a few years ago, when an inspired administrator, noticing that students spent a fixed number of hours in courses but received a variable grade, proposed an experiment in which they would spend a variable number of hours but get a fixed grade. To have completed the work of a course to the genuine satisfaction of all parties would merit an A; the student would stay in class just as long as it took to get his A. Something like this seems to me reasonable within the special field of the student's concentration, but outside it—at the other places on the map—the maximum that should be demanded of him is a signed, and if necessary sworn, statement that he has been there and does not plan to stay. He would leave the university, with a certificate saying that he could or could not profit from still further work in his area of concentration, just as soon as he had exhausted what the faculty in that area had to offer him. The highest university qualification would be an attested capability to *go on learning* when *all* institutional resources, including those of the university itself, had been fully taken advantage of. Such a qualification would certify a man as an autonomous and free agent in the domain of the intellect.

Entrance tests, curricula, grade averages, degrees and the like belong in fact not at all—or at least no longer— to the internal organization of the university as an institution of higher learning but to its external organization as as administratively efficient entity and to its function in the society at large. (I say "external" because whatever their original justification these things are now sustained by trustees, overseers, regents, professional organizations, non- (or ex-) academic administrators, and so on. They are also passionately defended, it is true, by faculty members attached to the status quo, who are afraid of losing their students under a less constrained system.) Their effect is to perpetuate a view of the hierarchical layering of society and of the need for overt marks of this layering, and the governance structure ministers to this view uncritically. The link I have been trying in a roundabout way to establish between goals and governance may now become clearer, for if it turns out that the perpetuation of this structure of society ought not to be one of its goals, and if it turns out that the goal of the efficient administrative organization of the university is incompatible with other goals more important to society—for example unrestricted access to the results of research, public understanding of science and art, the elimination of irrelevant and discriminatory criteria for employment, the training of humane and intellectually lively teachers—then the present scheme of governance of the university may prove not only to fall short of but also perhaps to be wholly irrelevant to the true goals of the institution.

I have worked out what I consider to be some of the desirable features of a university serving such true goals in two other publications ("Design for a University," *Daedalus,* Winter 1970, reprinted in Stephen R. Graubard and Geno A. Ballotti, eds., *The Embattled University,* New York:Braziller, 1970, and "Notes on a Visit to a Distant Campus," in Margaret Mahoney ed., *The Arts on Campus: The Necessity for Change,* New York, New York Graphic Society, 1970), so that I need not describe them further here. It remains to specify what those goals are. And for this purpose the university must be taken in the context of the rest of the educational system. The function of an educational system, as I see it, is to provide whatever in the way of education may be needed or desired in the society it serves. Education I take to be a *process,* a process that produces some change in the person submitted to it, so that he or she leaves the institution in which the formal parts of the process take place (the school, the university, the clinic, the prison) a different person from the one who entered it.

This is not the place to deal with the educational character of prisons and clinics (i.e. clinics for the physically disabled or the psychologically disturbed) although it is worth remarking as an aside that such institutions *obviously* belong to the educational system and will not be adequate to their purpose until they are fully integrated with it. The more familiar parts of the system fall into a four-part sequence of elementary school, high school, college, and graduate or professional school, the latter two stages jointly constituting the university. The input to the elementary school stage is a child who is physically independent (to a sufficient degree, during school hours) but pre-literate and morally and socially dependent, and its output, ideally, is a literate child who, while still dependent intellectually, practically, and emotionally, is morally and socially independent. Since the high-school stage customarily follows at once, its input is just the output from the elementary school; its output, again ideally, has become independent emotionally, practically, and intellectually, and furthermore is politically aware. (Note that, as argued above, the society is not functioning if on the one hand this is the age of political participation and legal independence, while on the other these criteria are not satisfied. Note also that it is entirely the job of institutions *below* the university level to see that the criteria are satisfied.) This is what the university should receive as input.

Now it will be said—it always is said—that this is an unrealistic estimate of the situation, that general education remains to be completed (in some cases started) at university entrance, and so on. And of course this is undeniably true. But we are still dealing with the goals of the university; and if the system to which the university belongs is so manifestly in a state of breakdown—and it manifestly is, as a glance at social, psychological and political conditions will show— surely the first order of business for the university is to mount a full-scale attack on the causes of this breakdown, rather than accommodate to it. In case it should be thought that social, psychological and political conditions are not evidence of a breakdown in the educational system, that the system is doing a pretty good job under the circumstances, etc., it may be worth stressing that every act of violence, every bureaucratic decision, every perpetuation of economic injustice, is in the end the result of an individual action or a set of individual actions, and that if an individual performs an action which has an adverse effect on society or another individual, his failure to do something better has only two possible explanations: a failure in genetics, or a failure in education. Education cannot perhaps be blamed for not having the knowledge or understanding requisite to a solution to the problem of immoral behavior, but it can be blamed for not making use of the knowledge we already have. The argument that other factors besides genetics and education—for example social conditions, economic inequalities, the breakdown of the family, etc.—are to be blamed is only an indirect way of saying that the education of *earlier* generations has failed. The short-range goal of the university ought, therefore, to be the creation of conditions under which it can function as a true university, and this means first of all attention to the rest of the educational system. And it is of course largely the university's fault if the rest of the system does not provide it with an input meeting the criteria specified above, since it itself has in fact provided the teachers and administrators whose work is supposed to have this effect.

The university does not seem to be collectively aware of the relation between its intellectual and organizational health and the health of the lower stages in the educational system. An awareness of this might produce two practical courses of action, both of which I propose as serious recommendations. First—since there is nothing incongruous in the university's taking concerted action on a wide front, even though this has hardly ever been done—the university system as a whole might call a moratorium, for a period of five years, say, on the production of any except the most indispensable new experts in specialized fields, and concentrate its entire attention on the production of teachers for the lower schools. Education is in such crisis that a national movement of this kind seems not inconceivable. It is not so much that there are not enough teachers in the schools, as that they seem to have forgotten, or perhaps to have misjudged, what a society like this requires of them. There are of course exceptional teachers, even exceptional school districts, but the gross evidence I have already appealed to is enough to show that a radical overhaul is needed. I envisage a situation in which a good proportion of the time of every university professor would be devoted explicitly to the question of what, in his subjects, the elementary or high school teacher ought to know, and what (if anything) he ought to teach to his pupils, in which graduate assistants or even professors would take up part-time teaching in the schools while the regular teachers went back for shorter or longer periods to the university, in which every effort of the imagination and will was directed in a coordinated way to solve the problems of the attractiveness of schools to pupils, of the morale of teachers, of the expectations of teachers with respect to pupils and of pupils with respect to themselves in matters of literacy and knowledge and perception, in which students of art would direct their attention to the appearance of the school environment, in which students of social problems would adopt school districts in connection with their field work, in which students and professors of psychology, economics and political science would engage in lobbying at the state and federal level for adequate funds for public education, and so on.

The second recommended strategy is more specific, and directs itself only to the interface between the high schools and the universities. University teachers are often heard to complain that students are delivered to them inadequately prepared for work at the university level, but they hardly ever do anything about this situation. The standard institutional response to poor preparation is remedial work of one kind and another, but an alternative response might be a protest, directed not at the student but at the school from which he comes. At present the interface between the high school and the university appears to be penetrated only by the student; there are counselors on the school side and admissions officers on the university side, and these people may know and work with one another, but the professional associations of high school and university faculties, even in subjects they teach in common, are segregated, and it is rare for a university professor, even one who teaches elementary courses, to know any of the teachers who taught his students their most advanced courses in high school. But if the latter have allowed a substandard product to get through (I employ the natural idiom of commerce as reflecting the impersonal way in which students are habitually labeled and forwarded) there might be some virtue in drawing their attention to the fact, and even of using this as a pretext, if no more friendly one could be found, for making their acquaintance. If university people were to make clear in what condition they wanted their students to come to them—if they had thought this out in specific terms, which is not often the case—it might turn out that the school people could do something about it that they were not as yet doing, not at all because of incompetence but just because they were not aware that it was needed.

If the kind of integration of the educational system that this breach of one of its watertight barriers represents were to take place, the university would finally be able to take up its proper mission, which is to provide for all those (of whatever age) who need and can profit from it an environment conducive to the higher learning, i.e. to a kind of learning that cannot be automatically produced by any combination of program, curriculum, and authority, the standard tools of teaching and training, but which requires resources and motivations of a different order. It would be able to do this in the knowledge that the students' needs in the way of teaching and training were taken care of elsewhere, even in some cases by means of institutional attachments to itself; it would in fact be part of a true educational *system*. One of the goals of the university must surely be the realization of such a system, in which the location and interrelation of the various parts would be mutually understood and exploited for the good of the society. In the present state of unsystematic, even chaotic, multiplicity of institutions with conflicting interests and goals it might be said aphoristically that the main goal of the university is to be a university. If it were one, how would it govern itself?

Well, it obviously *isn't;* the question may therefore, once again, seem Utopian. And yet the resolute intention to treat it as such might do as much as anything to make it so. At present we often do not treat our students as university students, nor our colleagues as university professors, not our Deans and Presidents as university administrators; we treat our students as children, our colleagues either as rivals or as fellow-employees, the members of the administration as managers or bosses. No wonder, if we cannot trust the people in the university to behave as if they were in one—if our model is the kindergarten or the factory or the corporation or even the state—that it does not look like a university. It has become commonplace to say that the university is a bureaucracy or a political structure, that its governance proceeds by conflict between centers of power and interest groups, and so on. These models are often opposed to another that is labeled the "community of scholars," which is condemned as unrealistic because the old isolation of the academy no longer obtains in the modern world, the university is involved with and must respond to the demands of a technological society, etc. But to be involved with something does not necessarily mean to substitute its standards for one's own.

The expression "community of scholars" is not, it is true, a very happy one, both because of the image it calls up and because of the inherent vagueness of its constituent terms. What people in universities, whatever their place in the community or their scholarly habits, might be *expected* to have in common is a commitment to knowledge rather than opinion, and to reason rather than emotion, as grounds for belief and action. Such people ought precisely to be in a position to transcend considerations of power and self- or group interest; the fact that they are not able to do so should if anything be a cause for shame, and not a fact of life to be accepted. If social scientists, taking a position of neutrality, observe that the behavior of people in universities is just as short-sighted and venal as that of people in any other institution, it is not a matter for surprise that the public—including the students themselves—should lose respect for the university and that legislators should feel free to attack it as an irrelevant luxury. The last thing we should do is to reflect these weaknesses in the governance structure by designing it as a cross between ward politics and cost-efficiency management. The governance plan of a university ought to be such that it works only if the virtues proper to a university are brought into play: if it fails it will have deserved to fail, since the institution will have ceased to be a university. It is not possible to save the university by turning it into something else.

It is at this point that I revert to the Marxist theory of the state, because in a somewhat oblique and somber way it carries a lesson for the university. As everybody knows, the Marxist theory of the state is that there ought to be no state; it ought to wither away, having been created only for the perpetuation of class differences and economic exploitation, the elimination of which makes it unnecessary. The functions of the state should be assured by the administration of a classless society. (Engels, the principal exponent of this theory, found an approximation to this condition in early revolutionary America at a time when "the free colonist predominated," but lamented that the rise of industrial capitalism made the emergence of a conventional state, with an armed police force and a military establishment, inevitable.) The emergence of this society would depend on a *prise de conscience* on the part of the working class, which, discovering its true humanity and cured of its alienation, would emancipate (after expropriating) the bourgeoisie also; this metamorphosis accomplished, a harmonious social order would result, in which the relations between men would be governed by mutual regard rather than by law. The only difference between the Marxists and the anarchists was that the latter thought this happy condition could be reached all at once whereas the former thought it would take a somewhat complicated historical preparation.

As everybody also knows, nothing like this has happened; in the places where the state, with its "special detachments of armed men," was supposed to wither away, it re-established itself in more virulent forms than ever. This failure of the theory has been due to two principal causes: the followers of the revolution did not rise to Marx's expectations, and its leaders fell into the usual temptations of power and affluence. The lesson for the university lies here. Ideally a university administration would be just that—it would administer the affairs of an academic society not divided into classes (students, junior faculty, senior faculty, and so on) and not disturbed by any competition (over funds or space, for example) whose roots lay in personal or professional interest. There would be no class except the class of intellectually committed adults, and no interest except the collective interest. To arrive at this state of affairs would require a *prise de conscience* on the part of all members of the university community that has not taken place. The other side of the coin lies in the lamentable fact that administrators, once in power, frequently count the perpetuation of that power among the legitimate objects of its exercise. We thus arrive at the University State, as it were, with its bureaucracy and its repression. The bureaucracy is obvious enough; the repression, while not sinister or deliberate, is nevertheless unfortunately real in terms of the coercion of spirit that overtakes too many students and faculty members at too many institutions.

Now it is not really surprising that the proletariat and the politicians were not equal to Marx's demands, but their failure need not be taken as final even in the world-historical sense, and it constitutes a positive challenge for the analogical case of the university. The academic *prise de conscience* might take place, is perhaps already beginning, and given the nature of the population concerned it might lead to collective action. The university might become classless, in the sense that the *formal* hierarchy of students, faculty and administration might wither away, to be replaced by a set of still asymmetrical but collaborative relations between faculty and students, and by an administration that only administered and did not also determine policy and wield power over the rest of the institution. And the way to make all this happen, I am suggesting, is to behave as if it *had* happened. If enough people, taking consciously into account what was involved, were to adopt this attitude, it *would* happen.

I do not wish to press the analogy further, certainly not to try to find strategic recommendations for university reform in the historical parts of Marxist theory. My purpose is served by showing the kind of human organization he thought eventually possible, and by suggesting that the university, precisely because it is not a fortuitous association of free agents but rather, as pointed out at the beginning, a deliberate association of responsible agents—so that it has a true end, not the myth of history but the reality of intellect—might be a place in which such an organization could be realized. I reject any historical scenario because I believe that the organization arises naturally out of the *prise de conscience* and that in the academic case even more than the popular one this cannot be programmed—that it arises more surely out of the *absence* of program but in the light of recognizable goals.

I suspect, in fact, that as far as the overall achievement of individuals or generations is concerned, conscious plans for the internal organization of education (curricular reforms, the convening of assemblies, etc.) make virtually no difference—that while one can choose to have an educated population or not, the form that that education takes really doesn't matter, and as a corollary that the more one fusses over it, the worse it gets (so that students have to educate themselves in spite of the system, as is so often the case now). Education may well be one of those things, like the language itself, like marriage customs, like table manners and fashions of dress, that belong to the unconscious of the society and that will change less because of conscious manipulation than because of a kind of historical working out of their own inner conditions and potentials. It will be affected by large scale public events, like the depression or Sputnik, and the expert will learn to tell what kinds of events are going to affect it. The latest is of course the war in Vietnam. But it will not be affected much by the attempts of self-appointed specialists to change it. If the analogy between language and education holds—and given that education is something that happens to everybody, and is in fact one of the forms of transition from infancy to maturity, and from one generation to the next, this seems to me highly likely—then the fate of Esperanto and all similar attempts ought to be considered with attention and respect. The job of the theorist of education, like that of the theorist of language, will be not to try to make the instrument work better by interfering with it directly, but to try to understand its workings and to put the fruits of this inquiry at the disposal of people who use it. They, in turn, may not at once become better speakers or better educators, but they may be able to avoid the imposition of certain forms of egregious error (like always putting a comma after "yet" at the beginning of a sentence, or computing grade point averages) on other people. And with this new modesty and new information may come a new awareness, the *prise de conscience* itself, based on an understanding of the situation and a realization of one's place in it.

But what has educational theory to offer? At the university level, really very little. It has hardly even begun to lay down its empirical foundations. Most studies of the university have concentrated on just those aspects of it which, according to the analysis I have been developing, are of least importance—internal politics, pedagogy, departmental structures, the complexities of managerial administration. I conclude by offering two sets of recommendations: first, of a number of things that I think ought to be looked at in an effort to illuminate the place of the university in the educational system, and second of some practical elements in the design of a university that would really treat itself as a university. First, then, some projects for eager researchers into higher learning:

1.    Longitudinal studies of individual students and faculty members in universities (there are hardly any).

2.    Longitudinal studies of apprentices, people who have been through various training programs rather than to the university, people in other countries who did not go to the university but who would have done so had they been in the United States.

3.    Inquiries into the conditions for learning which best suit people of different preparations, of different ages, and of different interests, with particular attention to the question whether the ages from eighteen to twenty-two, in the light of the other forms of development taking place at this time, are particularly suited for higher education.

4.    A search of the literature, not only for the principles explicitly laid down by observers and theoreticians of the educational scene but also for those implicit in biographical and autobiographical accounts, so that the perceptions of people who have suffered and written about education might be made of use. (In particular self-taught people, whose lives and letters often make surprising reading, might be considered seriously.)

5.    Investigations of the inhibiting factors on self-motivated learning—anxiety, boredom, preoccupation with other things—the likelihood of their incidence under various conditions, and the possibility of averting them.

In the absence of these and other empirical inputs, reported in a language with a fairly standard vocabulary (another project that needs work), firm conclusions are difficult. Such investigations may indeed be under way, but if so it is all too likely, as is to be expected in a pluralistic free-enterprise society, that they are being conducted by a number of different people in a number of different places, whose efforts are poorly coordinated and whose perceptions of the salient factors differ. It is as though one had several research centers in physics working out complex correlations between phenomena described by idiosyncratic terminologies, making theories on rather slim experimental bases about parts of the world which might or might not overlap with one another. Physics must have been rather like that at the time of Aristotle; it, however, has moved forward since, whereas the theory of education has made very few, if any, improvements on Plato. The practical recommendations which follow assume that in these circumstances common-sense plus a few moral principles, consistently applied, is just about as good as the best theoretical conclusion. The moral principles involved have been adumbrated earlier in this paper; they include the respect that one ought to have for adult members of one's own society, the criminal character of manipulation or indoctrination, and also a respect for the use of resources and a modesty in the assessment of one's own worth to the society (not at this point one of the chief virtues of academic administrators).

1.  Require all students, as a condition of entry to the university, to submit a statement, written by themselves, as to their reasons for wishing to enter. Admit all high school graduates who actually submit such a statement, whatever it says; it is the effort of writing it, and not its content, that counts.

2.  If any high school graduate on entry proves to be deficient in any auxiliary subject (English, mathematics, etc.) provide remedial training but lodge a protest with the school in question, preferably a personal one (a visit from a faculty delegation to the principal of the school, for example).

3.  Provide the remedial training spoken of in (2) in a training institute attached to but not properly a part of the university. Place all training programs of any kind in such institutes. Let the faculty members in these institutes work on a different teaching schedule from faculty members in the university proper.

4.  Remove all requirements for graduation except actual attendance in the university and a minimum level of achievement within major courses. Let the diploma take the form of a simple statement of time spent and material mastered.

5.  Get out of the student's way once he has taken himself in hand; require that he do this, and be what his status in the society is, namely, an autonomous agent. Get rid of all counseling except medical psychiatry.

Let the statements of requirements, to the extent that any remain, be clear; if a student cannot read the statement, send him to the remedial institute referred to above.

6.    On entry to the university, inform the student—by means of a seminar or course—what the resources of the institution are and what he can expect to get out of it. Do this honestly, and without resorting to cant phrases like "self-realization" and "liberal education."

7.    Abolish all administrative posts above the department level except those of President, Registrar, and Treasurer. Spend the money thus saved on providing the most comfortable environment possible for learning. Let it even be luxurious. The other paper-work of the university can be done by purely clerical officers, and should any major administrative problem arise that the President cannot handle himself it can be taken care of by a committee of the faculty.

8.    Make sure that *every* member of the faculty discharges some administrative (i.e. committee) responsibility. At the moment 10 percent of the faculty staff 90 percent of the committees. Make these responsibilities *real;* have them form part of the continuing operation of the university. This would provide virtually all the supplementary administrative time necessary; such tasks of Deans, etc., as are in fact indispensable would fall to committee chairmen, whose tenure of these chairmanships would rotate but who would work with permanent (non-academic) committee secretaries. If in doubt as to the wisdom of abolishing Deanships, Assistant Deanships, etc., conduct an inquiry in the following terms: ask each administrative officer other than the President, Registrar and Treasurer to describe in detail what would happen if his position were abolished and his records burned. Consider whether the dire consequences he would no doubt predict would in fact follow.

9.    Let the faculty do what it does best; if a man is good at something, let him offer a course in it; if no students enroll for such a course, let him offer one in the thing he is next best at. If he does not do anything well (and *knowing* something well is not in itself *doing* anything well) do not renew his contract. (Tenure is another story, and a more complicated one; I have made some recommendations about it in "Design for a University," but leave it aside here.)

10.    Operate on the principle that it does not matter what, in particular, a faculty member does, as long as he does it well, nor what in particular a student does as long as it engages his intellect at a sufficiently challenging level. (Note that everything that is challenging is interesting.) Let the course structure of the university find its own equilibrium in terms of what the faculty can supply and what the students demand. Remember, however, that the condition of intelligent demand on the student's part is that he should know what is available and how it relates to everything else

(see recommendation 6 above).

11.    Make available many short, well-written books, preferably paperbacks, and preferably gratis. It does not matter what they are about as long as they are short and well-written, shorter and better-written if possible. The point is to interest the student. Hide the long and badly written books. If a student discovers that he needs one he will ask for it.

12.    Encourage, but do not require, the faculty to become familiar with other forms of presentation of material than lectures and books. Have first-rate ancillary services in the way of libraries, film centers, etc.

13.    Again, encourage but do not require the faculty to know something about the psychology and potential of their own students. Let the free-market mechanism described above determine retention or dismissal of faculty members, using the criteria already implicitly used (research and publication, teaching large numbers of average students or small numbers of outstanding ones). The current criteria of publication and teaching, like the United States Constitution, are perfectly adequate except that they have never really been tried. To the extent that they are invoked at all, this is done with too much indulgence.

14.    If the course structure is retained, devise short sequences of interconnected courses (in different disciplines if necessary) which can fit on to one another like modules, and allow students to choose between one whole semester or whole year unit and another where possible rather than between individual courses.

15.    Break down the population of the university into units of faculty and students within which it is possible for everybody to know everybody. (In order to accomplish this, it is not necessary to build residential colleges. Consider the House system of the British public schools as adapted in government-supported schools, according to which each pupil on entry is assigned to an invisible "house" with which he is affiliated for purposes of intramural competition, etc. It would not be difficult to make such an institution a human and social reality.)

16.    Impose no residence requirement for any degree. Let people enter at whatever age they like, and for however long they like. As a corollary of this, encourage them to leave for a while as soon as they have had enough. If possible, abolish the degree altogether (see "Design for a University").

And what has become of governance in all this? Who votes, for example? Well, the design is not complete, but enough should have been said, between the meditations and the recommendations, to make clear that the whole point is to design governance *out* of the institution as far as possible, to make it anarchic in the strictest sense. My claim is that, if the university were operated with the intentions and on the principles I have adumbrated, it would survive with a much reduced administration and with much less fuss about governance, as well as becoming a far more human and agreeable place. People care about the structures of governance only when things are obviously wrong (a great deal of the motivation for the assembling of the Assembly mentioned at the beginning has already evaporated) and things are most likely to go wrong when the structures are too rigid and the goals of the institution too ambiguous. The thesis of this essay could be summed up by saying that clear goals and flexible governance are better than vague goals and rigid governance—but that the governance cannot become flexible unless the goals are clear. For completeness it is necessary to say that *if* a problem of governance arises, nobody in the university who is affected by it should be excluded from the deliberations about it. But by now—or at least let us hope soon—it should be possible for all of us to get on with our own work.

# Truth and Institutions: Reflections on the 125th Anniversary of the Smithsonian Institution

S. Dillon Ripley
Secretary, Smithsonian Institution
Washington, D.C.

That there is an Institution at all seems to be due to the persistence of John Quincy Adams, sometime President, who resumed his public career in the House of Representatives, and who, upon hearing of the legacy of Mr. Smithson to the Nation when his remaining heir died in 1835, resolved to dedicate himself to bringing the project to fruition. Adams was appointed chairman of a select committee to determine the matter. He quickly found that his task was not easy. John Quincy Adams was an eighteenth-century aristocrat who has been described by a recent historian as "the last nineteenth-century occupant of the White House who had a knowledgeable sympathy with the aims and aspirations of science or who believed that fostering the arts might properly be a function of the federal government."

His colleagues in the Congress thought he was out of step. They respected him but they did not have his vision. Besides they thought there was a catch in the terms of the bequest. As Adams noted in his diary, "Vail intimates . . . the man (Smithson) was supposed to be insane." "Bankhead thinks he must have had republican propensities" (which of course could have been probable). One of the Congressmen kept hoping that the courts would discover another illegitimate relative so as to give the whole mess back to England. Another Congressman said that the money simply should be returned to England forthwith. A Senator wanted it to be donated for a university and have himself named the first president for his own greater glory.

But Adams had a conviction—"the increase of knowledge" was not the same as education. Education in the United States was a solemn duty for the children and youth, so as to endow them as individuals with useful truths and knowledge already acquired, and suited to their respective condition. An education qualifies an individual for the enjoyment of his or her rights as a citizen, and for the performance of their duties throughout life. In effect, every man and every woman in this country has the right to be taught how to plow a straight furrow in life.

By accepting the Smithson Trust with its declared objects for the increase of knowledge, and having pledged its faith for the application of the funds to these purposes, the Congress would be derelict in its obligation not to sponsor and support research, in science and the arts. Only in this way could knowledge be increased.

With Adams as the visionary with the power to have his way eventually in the Congress, the extraordinary coincidence for this Institution was that Joseph Henry, an equally visionary scientist one hundred years ahead of his time, was writing from Princeton suggesting how the funds could be adapted for the advancement of science and culture. Henry was a twentieth-century scientist caught in the Nineteenth. He was as equally dedicated to basic research as Adams was convinced of the necessity of protecting the mission of the Smithsonian. The two together were indispensible for the success of the Institution, for their power and perseverance enabled it to follow a course in direct opposition to the prevailing pragmatism and practicality of the time. Joseph Henry became the first Secretary and never failed to point out in his early reports to the Congress, as if the life of everyone depended on it: "The Institution . . . is the establishment of an individual . . . to bear and perpetuate his name. The bequest is for the benefit of mankind. The Government of the United States is merely a trustee to carry out the design of the testator. The objects of the Institution are first, to increase, and second, to diffuse knowledge among men."

In Henry's interpretation, faithfully followed ever since, these two objectives are distinct. The first implies our sponsorship of basic research, the second our sponsorship of publications, and the widest possible communication and exchange of documents and information. Although Henry stated that all branches of knowledge are entitled to their share of attention, he continually specified that work should not be undertaken which could be more effectively produced elsewhere. Additionally he recognized the original mandate of the Congress to establish a library, a museum and a gallery of art. It was in these latter objectives that he eventually succeeded in obtaining an annual appropriation from the Congress for funds for maintenance and care of the public collections.

The increase of knowledge can and has been pursued in two ways. On the one hand original research has been sponsored for many years. In some cases the Secretary's own predilections have been followed. Henry, for example, felt that an understanding of the weather cycles in our vast domains was not only a worthy object of original research but when understood and correlated could be of signal benefit to the Nation. Once a basic understanding of weather cycles was achieved, then the second aspect of "increase" came into play. Meteorological tables could be constructed, methods of data recording as well as acquisition could be perfected, and finally the whole apparatus transferred to an applied bureau, a government bureau, where the work could be appropriately administered and funded for the benefit of all.

Similarly Secretary Langley sponsored the Institution's research in astrophysics, which continued to this day, has resulted in a vast body of basic research, particularly in the last fifteen years of our joint association with Harvard University. From basic research, the astrophysical observatory has branched into an active role in teaching, in applied research for NASA and other Government agencies, and finally in one of the ultimate rationales of all this, the "diffusion": the publication of standard tables, encyclopedic works, in our case works on geodesy and the measurements of the Earth, star catalogues and a compendium of information on stellar atmospheres. Thus one outgrowth of research follows complementarily: the publication of tables, of standards, of encyclopedic works. Nor must this aspect of research ever be downgraded or neglected, for without this cataloguing responsibility, much succeeding research would be impossible. Thus it has proceeded ever since: first research *per se* by individuals, second the publication of the catalogues. In this tradition, the Institution's century-old concern with documentation and record keeping as well as original ethnological and linguistic research on the American Indians has culminated in the assumption of the task of preparing the definitive twenty-volume Handbook of North American Indians which will be completed in 1976.

A hundred years ago, the Institution was preparing for the Philadelphia Centennial of 1876. The effects of that exposition were dramatic for the Smithsonian. We inherited a vast horde of objects, and the momentum of the acquisition was sufficient to bring us our second building, the Arts and Industries Museum, completed in 1878. Now, a hundred years later, this Institution is busily planning for the Bicentennial in 1976. In Washington, at least, we can concentrate on delineating the American experience for millions of visitors who will be thronging our Nation's capital in that year. We have a duty and an obligation to do so, not only to remind Americans and others of our past, the impact of our science, our technology, and yes also, our culture on our surroundings and on ourselves, but also through these legacies to discern the possibilities for our future. The projection of our past upon a screen, mirrored with the faces and the colors of the present, can surely be used, as in a camera lucida, to outline the traces of the future.

Who can be so foolish as to put away our past? No man of business in his right mind would overlook a past annual report. It is a travesty of our educational processes in these days of increasing complexity, of vast accumulations of facts and data, that the teaching of history is going out of fashion. The reason for it is not far to seek, and would cause any rational believer in the precepts of education such as John Quincy Adams to assume that we had taken leave of our senses. The teaching of history has been transformed by the teaching of sociology, so that today history is thought by young people to be a collection of myths interpreted through oracles. The oracles are influenced by priests who are thought merely to be 'selling' something. Therefore, none of it is necessarily true. All over the world whole segments of people have become used to systems in which lies are used as the basis for propaganda and policy. In such an atmosphere, enhanced by the instant communications which now subject us to so little opportunity for reflection or objective thought we realize that Adams' "useful truths and knowledge already acquired" are thought of as a very limited part of contemporary higher education. Theories have become more fashionable than facts. The existence of truth is doubted by skeptics, and the young feel that life is a "put on."

At the same time the truth exists in objects. It can be interpreted and understood through objects. They cannot lie. Perhaps objects have been classically revered for this reason. They can be handled, touched, thought about and reflected over, and in so doing convey a sense of the truth beyond peradventure. We know that the teaching of history is vital, we who care about objects. We know that the examples of history contain a reaffirmation of everything we believe in and hope for the future, whether it is in our own interest, that of our country, or that of our environment which is the world's. We know that the truth is contained in these things.

Why then does conventional, organized education pay so little attention to our kinds of research, to museum research, and above all to museum exhibits and education? If education as an industry is in difficulty, if there is a credibility gap brought on by an excess of skepticism, muddy thinking, outmoded ritual and a failure of belief, then I should think an effort to go back to first principles would be of the highest priority. A well-known Communist intellectual was recently quoted as saying, "After mature consideration I have come to the conclusion that the only revolutionary thing in the world is the truth." In the world today the truth is denied to many people. On our side of the fence it seems to us that perhaps one half of the world's population is so deprived. But the proportion can be said of course to be much greater. If the truth is really revolutionary it can be said not to lie in most established institutions, whether political or otherwise, including vast institutions of commerce which in themselves are like minor nations. We in America had prided ourselves for nearly two centuries on truth as an aspect of the pursuit of freedom, and happiness, in a free press, liberty of worship and a national attitude of mind which was endlessly enquiring. From this we produced miracles of technology, shrewd insights into manners of organization and trade and a sense of purpose—our belief in ourselves, our honesty and our idealism. Today's education has degenerated into a temporary transfer of training and information. Much of the best of it is disguised as trade-learning, but trades theselves are thought to be demeaning. Professionalism in education is largely a fanciful conceit for officialism. Much teaching today is time serving and produces anomie rather than endowing the student with any sense of purpose or "the enjoyment of his rights as a citizen" as Adams phrased it.

In the last three or four years this Institution, like other major institutional systems in our land, has come under scrutiny. Our purposes like those of the universities are questioned. Doubt and suspicion pervade our institutions, as people at all levels suspect the truth of what they hear and see and read. If we are a sacred cow as indeed we are, we should be capable of reaffirming our own goal to show the truth, to weigh all factors in the balance, not to be swayed by prejudice or bigotry whether it comes from the left or the right, but to diffuse knowledge objectively, to "tell it like it is."

It has been said by those perhaps too eager to claim such a distinction, people like university presidents for example, that a university is the sole instrument devised by men to illuminate and perfect the truth. A moment's reflection and the recollection of academic faculty debates should be enough to corrode one's confidence in such an illusion. No single institutional system or pattern could possibly claim the hegemony of a rational exposure of the truth. The truth is always too revolutionary, if you will. One can only strive for perfection but hardly ever assume that it is attainable.

If the Smithsonian is to increase knowledge in the next twenty-five years, let us join with others in using the Bicentennial observance as a means of reviving interest in the truth as expressed in objects. Let us continue our pursuit of the unfashionable by the unconventional. Let us relive the American experience to remind us of our hard won birthright and to point the way to the enjoyment of our rights as citizens of the world, in that world's only environment, our temporary home, our sole stopping place short of the stars. Let us also join with others in pioneering studies on the creation and capturing of interest, on studies in cognition, on the ability to learn effectively, so that all of us, men and women of a country in which we believe truth stil resides, can eventually achieve that age-old dream of our land, to be qualified through education for the enjoyment of our rights and for the performance of our duties throughout life.

# Regaining the Policy Initiative in the Modern University

Philip C. Ritterbush
Chairman, ORGANIZATION::RESPONSE
Washington, D.C.

The organization of the modern university and its involvements have compromised its ability to set policy for itself and called into question long-accepted ideas of academic freedom and institutional integrity. Following a survey of changes in the character of policy in the university this paper will sketch some of the foundations upon which academic policy might be reestablished.

Institutions of learning are constituted elements of the social order, characterized by their persistence over time and their capacity to induce a similarity of interests on the part of their members. Institutions are here considered as discrete entities rather than broad categories of social activity such as religion or property. The word institution derives from *statuere,* to set up, which presupposes that institutions are established for one or more governing purposes. It is so that institutions may pursue such chosen objectives that they are granted powers through a charter conferred by the parent society, customarily allowing them to operate without interference and safeguarding continuity in their efforts over time. Without some such warrant of freedom they could not construe their own calling.

Policy within an institution is the relation of the functions it performs to its objectives, whereby the activities it conducts are considered as means to the ends which distinguish the institution. Policy serves to translate institutional objectives into the context of everyday efforts. Policies may be consciously prescribed as a regulatory code, such as premises for the planning of facilities and programs, or they may be tacit guides to action that are unwritten and unspoken.

Medieval building forms and architectural styles were used in spite of their cost and inconvenience by colleges and universities until quite recently. The avowed purpose of traditional academic architecture was to evoke respect for learning but it served another purpose that now seems equally important, if less immediately obvious. By reference to self-sufficient medieval communities the gothic campus symbolized the institution's withdrawal from society in order to devote itself to serving its members. The elaborate gates and fences which surround so many colleges derive from the walls of fortress settlements. They mark clear limits to the institution, which is "localized" upon its site, to use the term introduced by Walter Metzger.[1] Such a life apart, chosen so that institutions might devote themselves to their chosen purposes, has been a characteristic feature of their existence. So monastic communities and manorial estates maintained self-sufficiency in order to protect their distinctive aims from compromise with a chaotic outside world. For establishments of this kind, insulation from society was the mainstay of policy.

The campuses of universities traditionally insulated them from society and reflected the self-sufficiency they enjoyed. These institutions usually succeeded in maintaining distinctive routines and in fostering a sense of community among their members, including belief in codes of conduct that were enforced among themselves so that resort to outside authority was hardly ever needed. The leadership of such institutions was commonly authoritarian in character, able to enforce policy in every context. Consequently such institutions enjoyed almost perfect freedom to plan their future activities, as a monastery might assign tasks to novices or an estate gradually extend its orchards and gardens. Plans could be carried out free from external interference or support so long as they did not exceed available resources. Within such self-sufficient institutions policies could be reviewed and enforced from a single point, were hardly ever subject to challenge from without, and consequently prescribed the future with assurance.

Today no university stands apart from its society. Policies can no longer be legislated from within. The features that most distinguish the modern university as an institution have worked great changes in the context of policy, which now differs radically from the institutional self-sufficiency that was once its precondition and premise.

# ONE. THE EROSION OF POLICY

## Shared Power: Policy and the Process of Governance

The administration of Columbia University by Nicholas Murray Butler has been called manorial, and one wag has styled Yale under Kingman Brewster a Gaullist institution. But today the power to make policy in educational institutions is shared among constituencies. A board of trustees commonly acts on behalf of the parent society. While it has a wide range of concerns, the items on its formal agenda tend to be those with a bearing upon the guiding purposes of the institution—those for which it was chartered. These objectives are to be applied, rather than altered, by its principal officers, as they work in planning, development, administration, external relations, resource allocation, and staffing. Of course their decisions commonly have a policy component, whether stated or not. In many institutions the pattern of decision by principal officers is as much policy as there is. Sometimes that pattern is considered and carefully drawn, even though never articulated in formal terms. When it comes to the actual performance of the functions of an institution by far the greatest part is played by its members. Some would say that officers should do no more than provide a setting for the activities performed by an institution's members. In their day-to-day activities the faculty and other staff members of a university, as well as their students, contribute directly to the institution's objectives. Indeed, objectives will be exceedingly abstract if they are not a direct expression of the personal and professional aspirations of an institution's members. Without in any way denying this vital personal dimension of institutions, one may still delineate a hierarchy of governance: uppermost are institutional objectives as determined by its founder and trustees; below these come policies serving those objectives as developed by the officers; and on a still lower level come the activities by which the members of an institution perform its functions.

The different constituencies of the university are rarely united in a common view of any policy question. An issue that students or faculty perceive in terms of their immediate experience of learning or teaching is transmuted into a legal or financial issue when it reaches the officers, and should it be considered by the trustees they may see it in light of some long-standing difference of opinion among themselves. Guiding objectives, administrative strategies, and everyday professional activities are three horizons of policy. Like a three-part prism they break a single image into three and project a multiplicity of images from a sequence of events. Perhaps the most formidable obstacle to precise rationality of policy in institutions of learning is their organization into constituencies oriented toward different aspects of policy in a way that prevents issues from coming into focus.

## Incompatability in Functions

Several commentators have noticed that the modern university is indebted to the German university for its traditions of research, to Oxford and Cambridge for its ideals of undergraduate education, and to the history of the American land-grant colleges for its conceptions of public service. Universities commonly cite research, education, and public service as their primary functions. They do not, however, expect each function to be conducted so as to reinforce the others or even be in harmony with them. These different functions evolved in parallel rather than in true interdependence. Humanists, generalists, and undergraduates may conceive the educational function as paramount. Scientists, specialists, and graduate students may think the research function should have primacy. Those in professional schools or of activist temperament may wish to see the public service function predominate. Clark Kerr remarks, "These several competing visions of true purpose, each relating to a different layer of history, a different web of forces, cause much of the malaise in the university communities of today." [2] It is not that these functions are inherently at odds with one another, but that institutions perform them without standards regulating the extent to which each would be expected to reinforce the others, for the institution as a whole or within its smallest units of organization.

## Cohesion and Entrepreneurship

Once he has fulfilled his departmentally prescribed teaching obligations the typical university faculty member seeks to invest his time for maximum professional and personal return. It is still a rare university that can sustain more than the incidental expenses of research or pay the costs of travel undertaken to develop instructional offerings. For projects of this kind outside support must be found, usually through research or consulting agreements with external sponsors who have aims of their own, differing in some measure from the faculty member's original intention. As the terms for sponsored research must be negotiated by the individual faculty member, because he is the most knowledgeable about the substantive aspects of the work to be done, the parent institution caters to feelings of professional integrity and surrenders much of the control it might otherwise seek to exercise over the scope and character of the work to be performed.

The Federal Government is virtually the sole source of research support. Fedral funds for academic science and technology constitute more than three-quarters of the operating budget of several technical universities and over half the operating budget for a number of major research-oriented universities. Support is offered for the institution as a whole only in a few inconsiderable programs. There has also been in the last few years a tendency for federal agencies to try to intervene more actively in work in progress in order to realize certain "targeted" objectives of their own or coordinate the efforts of investigators who seem to be doing closely related work. The sponsored research system has never lacked apologists but it has never been studied systematically for its impact on institutions. Recently the Council of the Princeton University Community undertook a sustained study of the impact of sponsored research on the university, directed by physicist Thomas Kuhn. "If the sponsored research system had originally been conceived for the multiple purposes it has come to serve," they concluded, "it would have been very differently designed." Their report offers valuable reflections on institutional integrity, which are quoted in the two following paragraphs.

> Two sorts of dangers result, and they are not everywhere merely potential. The first is to balanced growth. Most or all universities have used some funds released by sponsored research to promote development in non-supported fields, but growth of faculty, staff, and facilities has usually been far more rapid in fields for which external support was readily available. Differential development of that sort need not be an evil. Selective financing is a classic way of expressing society's values, and universities ought not be immune to them. But decisions about university growth ought nevertheless to remain deliberate and considered responses to new opportunities rather than, as has sometimes been the case, to the mere availability of funds. Institutional control has, in any event, often been difficult to maintain because of the critical role played by individual faculty research preferences in the search for funds . . .

> The second main danger posed by the funding system is to the balance and integration of a university's teaching and research functions. Partly to increase the quantity of research and partly to compete for the rare faculty members who do it best, the growth of research support has been accompanied by a reduction of teaching loads, especially marked in the departments which can attract research funding. More important—perhaps the most striking effect of the system—has been the proliferation on many campuses of non-teaching research institutes which make little or no contribution to

the teaching function. . . . Change has almost everywhere been evolutionary, an unconscious institutional response to an altered environment, rather than a consequence of deliberate choice. The process has too often been drift rather than decision. . . . We urge scrutiny at the first appropriate time of the organization of the funding system from which the principal external pressures on universities currently derive.[3]

## Commitments and Resources

On an income of one pound Sterling per week, noted Mr. Micawber, one can be a pauper if one spends twenty-and-six, or get along quite well if one spends only nineteen-and-six. One shilling in twenty makes all the difference and the problem is one of control of commitments. In the university a system of allotments to schools and departments is employed for each fiscal year. This is a fairly effective way of distributing income but it does not prevent these units from conceiving responsibilities for themselves that outstrip available resources. The advent of computers, for example, may confront a university not only with demands for expensive facilities and hardware, but also with proposals for a department of computer science, enlargement of the philosophy department to include a specialist in symbolic logic, new courses in statistical methods in the social sciences, new appointments in electrical engineering or applied physics, and special programs in mathematics. To their respective schools and departments these all seem to be legitimate needs. And so they are, but to the institution whose philosophy department seemed adequate without a specialist in symbolic logic the need may come as an abrupt surprise. And if the new appointment is made, in its wake will follow requests for new library acquisitions, extensions in the program of instruction, admission of graduate students with new and different interests, and needs for more sophisticated equipment. None of these needs was open to prior review and decision by university authorities. They follow directly from established principles of university organization but they represent the creep of events rather than anyone's considered judgment, much less an advance plan. An increase in course requirements for a major, the publication of a costly new reference work, the "sophistication" of laboratory equipment—all serve previously recognized program interests but are certain to be presented as claims for new resources.

University budgets do not usually relate expenditures to underlying commitments or to the performance of specified tasks. Instead they apportion estimated university income among departments and other units, making it almost impossible to know in any detail how the funds are used. A further difficulty is that actual expenditures follow authorization by up to two years.

### Professional Styles and Cultural Identities

There are wide differences in professional outlook and attitude within any university community. The texture of knowledge is not uniform. There are some who weave patterns and others who unravel tangled skeins of prior supposition. Experimentalists tend to speak a common language irrespective of their field of specialization. Those working in descriptive fields commonly prefer a more solitary habit of thought as opposed to workers on rapidly moving frontiers of theory, who seem forever to be comparing notes and interacting at high levels of personal energy. Faculty members whose studies involve the evaluation of society tend to share liberal political attitudes while those most concerned with industrial research and production commonly evince a more conservative outlook.[4]

A recent survey of faculty members in six colleges, conducted by Jerry Gaff and Robert Wilson of the Center for Research and Development in Higher Education at Berkeley, showed consistent differences among faculty categories. Social scientists and humanists favored social and personal activism while natural scientists and those in professional schools were much less receptive to controversial activities. Instructors in engineering and mathematics discouraged classroom discussion, which was encouraged by those in philosophy, religion, and history. Those conducting the survey concluded that natural scientists, humanists, social scientists, and faculty in professional or applied fields constituted distinctive cultures, reflecting differences in preparation or professional interests.[5]

Perhaps the term "culture" implies greater cohesion and distinctiveness than are to be found in actual fact. But these observers have identified a principle of human dynamics in institutions that operates quite consistently. Individuals of similar psychological makeup exhibit certain predispositions on policy questions and will often draw together into customary alliances in ways that greatly obscure their points of view.

Another fundamental cleavage within many institutions is that which separates professional and academic interests from administrators. Financial and support services, even those dealing with the human interests of the institution such as personnel, guidance, and community relations, are divorced from the academic enterprise they are meant to serve. This is a fruitful source of factionalism.

Its power divided among constituencies, its functions at odds, unable to regulate the interests of its members or the commitments they entail, the modern university differs greatly from the simpler, self-sufficient institutions of an earlier era. It is governed not by policy but by consensus. Its members contend against one another with very different conceptions of its allegiences, irreconcilable claims upon resources, and can agree on little more than their mutual reluctance to entrust the university as an institution with the power to decide matters of substantive import.

As the forces of institutional cohesion weakened, the university came to be viewed as a pluralistic composite. Its professional members insisted on the freedom to pursue their individual interests without fear of being over-ridden by authority. Decisions regarding staffing, finance, and academic program were decentralized to schools and departments. Areas of neglect have been remedied on an *ad hoc* basis by creating institutes or special programs, but coherence overall has become unattainable.

The Balkanization of the university does not trouble many who will concede organizational weakness in theory because they think in practice its disadvantages are largely offset by the wisdom and good faith of department chairmen and deans who forestall serious imbalances before they become disabling and somehow make an unwieldly system work. So long as one has good men in key positions, the argument runs, the institution should be able to maintain its equilibrium. Besides, the sheer complexity of the institution necessitates the establishment of specialist domains for decisions that cannot be properly understood, much less challenged, from other sectors of the institution. While it has lost organizational tidiness and sharply focused policies, the modern university has nonetheless gained substantial public influence, widened the range of its programs, expanded enrollment, and gained access to vast new resources. From this perspective the idea of an institution governed by distinctive objectives may seem unrealistic.

## TWO.  SOME POTENTIAL SOURCES FOR POLICY

Consider, as an example of a statement of objectives, the following profession of the aims of Princeton University:

1.  The education of undergraduate, graduate, and postdoctoral students.

2. The advancement of knowledge through research and scholarship.

3. The preservation and dissemination of knowledge.

4. The advancement and protection of the public interest and public welfare.[6]

Such a statement allows for all that men of good will would have the university do. It has permitted luxuriant growth and lavish activity, and led to splendid service to the public. The statement is not a specification of the objectives which distinguish Princeton as an institution but a list of the functions it performs. It cannot serve as a basis for policy because it cannot frame choices or lead to any conclusion about priorities. At the very least a statement of objectives would have to provide a framework for relating institutional resources to the purposes they serve.

Having enumerated some of the practical difficulties that beset policy and raised the question of whether an institution may do better without policy than with it, I would like to explore four aspects of the modern university which may show that there is at least a possibility for policy despite the obstacles in its path.

## Leadership and Integration

Robert Hutchins defines institutional leadership as the clarification, definition, proclamation, and enforcement of a distinctive "vision of the end" for which the institution exists.[7] But the leader of a modern university can do little more than orchestrate its responses. Certainly he is unable to prescribe a plan to be fulfilled. It is possible neither to define nor to maintain an internal community of interests. The university has become an internally inconsistent complex of facilities and activities. Its power is fragmented among numbers of ill-defined subsystems, which are allied with various external interests. It has become impossible for the occupant of this office to impose his will on the institution he heads. The external allegiances of virtually every sector of the modern university preclude a tidy conception of institutional leadership. As Clark Kerr observes, "There are more elements to conciliate, fewer to be led. The university has become the multiversity and the nature of the presidency has followed this change."[8] About all that a leader seems able to do is mediate competing interests while presiding over the introduction of innovations.

Despite this chastening description of the office of the presidency, its incumbent has the indisputable advantage of being one individual. In some of the most highly complex fields of litigation the best way to frame issues is for a single judge, sitting without a jury, or a master in equity, to study a case in all its ramifications so as to gradually evolve a single judgment. In somewhat the same way the administrative process provides for a hearing examiner who may take volumes of testimony and then present findings and preliminary statements of policy to a regulatory commission. As an officer of the court he is fully accountable for his treatment of the facts and interpretations of law.

The president of a university is obliged to partake of its full life as an institution—to immerse himself in personalities, finances, housekeeping, and planning. He may experience a mysterious fusion of his own identity with that of the institution he serves. If the institution does not draw upon his capacity to integrate his experiences it may fail to perceive aspects of institutional unity that could be revealed in no other way. Fred deW. Bolman points out in his study, *How College and University Presidents Are Chosen* (1968) that half of the presidents do not participate in any serious discussion of the primary aims of the institutions over which they will preside before assuming office. In a study of planning and governance in nine institutions, *Conformity* (San Francisco: Jossey-Bass, 1969), Warren Bryan Martin demonstrates for at least some colleges and university presidents that they rarely have the opportunity to apply what they know in formulating policy. Their time and that of other principal officers is generally consumed by short-term measures to relieve the institution from pressure.

No one today would maintain, as in Emerson's phrase, that an institution is the lengthened shadow of one man. Yet circumscribed as it is, the presidency of the modern university offers a potential for understanding the institution that rarely finds an outlet. Paradoxical though it may be to observe, the presidential office must be reasonably strong in order to develop policies that may transcend accidents of personality so as to express the fundamental life of the institution. If no effort is made to encourage such policies to emerge, the president, no matter how forceful he appears, will deal with details and the institution will enjoy little more than the illusion of leadership.

### Avoiding the Institutional Costs of Decentralized Resource Decisions

Much university income is tied to schools and departments, which receive it as tuition or as yield on investments. Sponsored research funds, apart from indirect costs, are typically spent without central review. Thus universities delegate control over these resources to schools or departments. Harvard University's capital funds yielded $36.3 million in operating income in 1968-69, but of this only one-tenth was available for university-wide functions as opposed to those of constituent schools that had long been accustomed to regarding endowment income as their own. The expectation has been that each unit of the university would retain gifts and tuition in order to finance itself. This principle of decentralization, stated in the hoary phrase, "every tub on its own bottom," rules out institution-wide policies regarding the use of resources. "It is fair to say that the present shape of Harvard reflects some 300 years' worth of bargains between generations of presidents, deans, professors, and administrators, on the one hand, and donors on the other." [9]

Decentralization encourages various elements of the university to seek funds on their own. This strategy may have been appropriate during the period from 1950 through 1968 when new governmental programs were proliferating. But it prevents the central authorities of universities from knowing how costs of similar activities compare among different elements or how central services relate to the institutional functions performed by the various schools and institutes. While this may not appear as a handicap when expenditures are steadily rising, under the changed conditions of today members of the university are likely to insist that resources available for the whole institution (even if these are only a fraction of all resources) be allocated according to the merit of various instructional, research, and support activities. Increasingly often the university will face internal demands that financial means must be in keeping with institutional ends.

Decentralized financial management involves the assumption that the functions carried out by elements of the university are ends in themselves: that all time spent in research is of equivalent value to the institution, or that the same is true of each credit hour of instruction. The role of policy, as we have defined it, is to relate an institution's functions to objectives. Functions are not in and of themselves the ends which distinguish the institution. Different *classes* of institutions perform different functions, but as universities are a class or subclass of institutions, all performing the same functions, they would be indistinguishable from one another in the terms we are considering unless they differed in their objectives as institutions. If for any reason whatever the university can no longer maintain a decentralized system of resource allocation it must legislate priorities which reflect institutional policies or preferences, to be applied to decisions about development, expenditure, and allocation. In almost all institutions such decisions are in fact taken, but usually behind a facade of consensus that conceals the complex processes of bargaining and compromise by which they were reached. Thus there exist *de facto* splinters of policy that might be brought together into a pattern of one sort or another. Sometimes the constraints upon the institution—such as a shortage of dormitory space, if identified, can be expressed as a policy favoring nonresident students, to give one example, even though there might be alternatives such as evening classes, extension activity, or televised instruction, that were not considered. Both constraints on resources and decisions about allocation can be translated into policy terms by those alert to their implications.

## Toward Coherence in the Institution's Response to Its Environment

Universities are truly distinguishable from one another by facts of place, even though some draw students from almost all nations or various regions of their own countries. No one has ever provided a good description of the relations between an institution of learning and its social environment. In ecological terms the niche structure of the setting of an institution of learning is so complex that it possibly exceeds the capacity of any one individual to understand. The advantage that institutions enjoy over individuals is that they can incorporate and build upon individuals' responses over long periods of time. They respond to their environment as a population rather than as an individual, somewhat as a tribe may occupy a valley. It is the role of tradition or even of conscious strategy to guarantee that advantageous discoveries are passed on, that exposures once found unprofitable will not be repeated, and that suitable customs will be nurtured. By cultivation, hunting, and civil engineering the tribe gradually transforms its physical setting. Where the interactions with the environment are adaptive the tribe flourishes and its setting improves. If opportunities are neglected and resources squandered the survival of the tribe is called into question or it may become subordinate to a more successful competitor.

The adverse environmental impacts of an institution may accumulate unnoticed until there is an explosion—as at Columbia, which offered the cruel spectacle of an institution that prided itself on its awareness of the character of urban life suffering heavily from the antagonisms of its neighbors and the depradations of law enforcement agencies.

One of the cultural tasks confronting our generation is to develop a rationale for the environmental relations of all units of society. Institutions of learning cannot escape this imperative. Few would wish to do so. Most recognize obligations to serve the various communities of which they are a part. Without the guidance of policy their responses will be uncoordinated and makeshift. There will be no way to appraise the institution's overall response to available resources, opportunities, or needs. Unless an institution has some systematic way to assess its impact it runs the risk of being excluded from desirable activities by competitors and failing to take advantage of worthwhile involvements.

Washington, D.C. is a challenging example of the complexity of the environments in which institutions of learning must function. Governmental and research establishments, museums, associations, and international organizations offer an extraordinary wealth of skilled professionals and interesting activities. They may serve somehow to exclude the area's educational institutions from niches they might otherwise occupy, for neither the private nor the public institutions of Washington had attained the status of "centers of excellence" by the 1960's, when that was being touted as the standard to which all should aspire.

The lack of a "first class university" in the Nation's Capital has been deplored by many academics, especially those coming to the area to serve for short times in governmental positions, whom one suspects to be hankering after a fresh student audience for last year's seminar. The reasons commonly cited are the lack of local patronage, because of the transient mentality of potential donors and so many professional workers; the displacement of industry or communications by a dominant Federal Government; or, one I have tended to favor, the fragmentation of the intellectual enterprise of the region into too many research institutes, museums, and universities with small graduate programs, in the absence of habits of interinstitutional cooperation. Each explanation has its counterpart in the theory of environmental biology, that might explain the character of an ecosystem in terms of diminished resources (why there is little life in open tropical seas), the dominance of some species displacing others (as the starling, pigeon, and English sparrow have done in cities), or excessive competition (as in some island populations). The ecology of institutions has not reached a stage of comparable certainty regarding the principles of environmental dependence or their application to cases.

Several years ago I embarked on an effort to monitor lectures, exhibits, concerts, symposia and similar events wherever they occurred in the Washington metropolitan area, and also to collect information on the academic interests of the professional population, including the faculties of all area universities, which were entered by broad disciplinary categories in an automated name and address retrieval system. A weekly *Washington Academic Calendar* was issued as the incentive for these individuals to participate in the system. Our hopes for a pioneer effort in monitoring the pattern of intellectual events in a city went aground on the reef of rising printing costs and the unwillingness of sponsored research agencies to fund something so unimportant as a system for measuring institutional aspects of the city's intellectual life.

If the institutions of a metropolitan area could be joined in a systematic effort to monitor their interactions with elements of the surrounding community and with one another, a great deal might be learned about their response to opportunity and their impact on society. Information about the external effects of institutions might be correlated with measurements of the functions performed, in order to generate suggestions about avenues of policy to be explored. The institution that fails to do so risks becoming the victim of environmental conditions that might have been turned to its advantage.

Finally, the social environment of each institution is composed of individuals, whom it may either serve or ignore. Many institutions have conducted their activities in patterns which their near neighbors consider discriminatory. Patterns of exploitation or neglect may have arisen unconsciously. The university may be unaware of them. But its neighbors often think otherwise and accuse the institution of pursuing deliberate policies aimed at them. To be hated for pursuing exploitive policies is the bitter dividend of failure to have any policies at all. It is perhaps in some ways to the credit of civic groups and others that they cannot believe that a great university can be drifting haphazardly and unaware. Those who find it bearing down on them may have to invent a helmsman in order to fix blame but they will hardly accept that something so vast and powerful as a modern university is out of control.

## Resuming the Dialogue over Institutional Purpose

Faculty and students share interests in the curriculum as a whole that transcend their experience of individual courses. Yet discussions of educational policy tend to be sterile or embarrassing. Sometimes there is a mood of confrontation, as in angry exchanges over language requirements. The overall shape of the curriculum receives remarkably little attention, although one might suppose it to be a matter of overwhelming interest to all concerned. This may be due to the opacity of the philosophical language used to classify or otherwise to describe knowledge or to the tedium of debates over method. It seems to me more likely to betray a reluctance to disturb delicate inter-departmental agreements as well as some fear that the structure of the institution's academic program cannot withstand examination.

It may be that much of the sense that the university is a mosaic of unrelated individual efforts results from a failure to look for interactions or common ground. For one thing, within the same institution the claims of one's colleagues are likely to receive more courteous attention than similar requests from outside the institution. One can ask an anthropologist about motifs in ancient art or a geographer about some aspect of urban history in hopes of being able to confirm the existence of some suspected relation between their subjects and one's own work. Being able to consult others about one's ideas while they are still tentative, while one is still soft-shelled after discarding a previous idea, is a privilege of enormous value. What is it that induces such tolerance for another person's intellectual novelties? Do we not have here some thread of common interest that might be picked up and followed? There may be other threads of policy lying about, from which a few fragments of fabric could, with a little effort, be woven. What may be lacking is an appropriate forum for integrative activity and any way of translating its conclusions into policy.

## THREE. FOUNDATIONS OF POLICY IN THE MODERN UNIVERSITY

Today's university resembles a city more than a monastery. A number of traditions survive within it side by side and it derives much of its vitality from their intersections. It draws students, staff, and visitors from the whole world. A true map of its involvements would show them extending far beyond the nucleus of its campus(es), rivaling a city in complexity and extent. Like a city it has its quiet neighborhoods, rundown or neglected areas, and foci of growth. The qualities that distinguish the university arise within it rather as a city gains its distinctive attributes: a sense of place, cultural traditions, concentrations of intellectual strength, and ties to other institutions. It combines such resources as a physical plant, permanent and transient residents, and reference systems in concentrated patterns that favor knowledge and its extension.

The primary orientation of the university is toward knowledge. More than any other institution the university determines the content and defines the limits of knowledge. It is the agency through which knowledge is transmitted from one generation to the next. Whatever receives its sanction may be regarded as knowledge. The establishment of science coincided with its adoption in universities. When secure knowledge of modern literature became possible its study was given academic standing, but not before it had attracted a sufficient intellectual endowment.

Although the occult and the future preoccupy many and are definitely of intellectual interest they are not admitted as subjects of study because knowledge of them is not, at least so far, capable of attainment. As its name makes plain, the university aspires to represent, through its faculty and reference systems, all knowledge in its chosen province. Institutions may embody a great deal of learning, as do the Bell Telephone Laboratories and the Huntington Library, but not be universities, not because they do not perform functions of education and public service in addition to research, but because they are not committed to extending knowledge across a broad front. Knowledge may be extended by discovery, instruction, or application, so the verb subsumes the three functions of universities.

The extension of knowledge to students or through applications is a social process. The student who consults reference books in private serves to extend knowledge, as does the inventor who affords it new contexts. Some of the acute policy problems of the modern university arise from the changing social context of knowledge. About one-quarter of the adult population is college-educated rather than one-thirtieth as was true between the Wars, and the aim of instructional programs in 1980 will be to convey knowledge to one-half of the adult population. What was economically or culturally desirable for three percent of the population is not going to be of equivalent value for fifty percent. Like medical care, literacy, adequate nutrition, the arts, or even central heating, knowledge has ceased to be a luxury good for an elite and has "gone public"—a decisive transformation of both knowledge and society, whose consequences are still unappreciated, even within the universities that have been primary agents in the process.

At the same time that knowledge is borne by more people than ever before it has found countless new applications to social needs. For about one-sixth of the work force, classified as professional or technical by the U.S. Bureau of the Census, the application of knowledge is their principal vocation. Virtually every enterprise of the society, from defense to social services, agriculture to local government, employs knowledge. It has become the indispensable public utility of our time, as was communication in the immediate postwar period, energy earlier in the century, or transportation a century ago. The result has been to transform the university into a pervasive system of services. A map of the university would resemble charts of railway networks or power systems, which show not just where their services are performed but also how goods or energy circulate in the society as a whole. This is not to say that the university should no longer accommodate the disinterested search for knowledge or the endeavor to transmit the best that has been thought and said to another generation. The purest forms of knowledge have their place, and it is an exalted one, in the social system of knowledge.

Like the traditional public utility, to take an electric power company as an example, the university can supply energies that are vital to the society, but it must also respond to external demand. Its officers are responsible for a network of existing facilities and staff that must be employed for their useful life. They must also be concerned to develop new and more effective sources of energy. And they must satisfy unexpected demands whose origins lie beyond their control, just as an electric utility must serve new communities and unexpected industrial innovations.

The transformation of the university has not been attended by an adequate conception of planning. There have been successful quantitative plans for the growth of institutions, such as those that every utility system must have. But we have crossed the threshold of a more complex phase of institutional development, again not unlike that which faces the electric utilities, which are now being forced to recognize that *balance* in the use of energy resources must take priority over expansion in consumption. Social interests not being well served by knowledge, such as environmental quality and the maintenance of community values, must be taken into account. University planning thus becomes a component of social development, as has long been true of planning by other utilities.

Once knowledge is seen as a social utility the vision of the university as a self-sufficient community disappears altogether. It is succeeded by an awareness that the cultural mission of the university is derived from the society as a whole. In the words of a statement issued by the University of the Witwatersrand, "Every civilized society tends to develop institutions which will enable it to acquire, digest, and advance knowledge relevant to the tasks which, it is thought, will confront it in the future. Of these institutions, the university is the most important."[10] The university transmits and criticizes the cultural heritage of society (including the legacies of ethnic groups not previously so served). It aids in the application of what is known and trains in skills derived from knowledge. Its investments determine directions in the search for knowledge thought to be of future value.

*The cardinal objective of any university is to represent the structure of knowledge in the composition of its faculties and their activities in research, teaching, and public service.*

No university can represent the structure of knowledge in its entirety. While the study of classical language and literature no longer attracts as much scholarly attention as it once enjoyed it still figures in the universe of knowledge and all but a few specialized universities make provision for it. Across the wide spectrum of knowledge each institution will at any given moment be active only in certain bands, some with special intensity, revealing a characteristic pattern like that of a spectrograph.

Every institution exercises choice about areas of the spectrum wherein it will concentrate and the extent of its intellectual range. These choices need not always be deliberate or at the institution's own initiative. The configuration of the institution's intellectual effort is the cumulative effect of years of decisions about departmental organization, staffing, and curriculum. Insofar as the institution has determined how and to what extent it seeks to represent knowledge, policies may be brought to bear upon the appointment of professional staff, the development of reference resources, and the conduct of a program of instruction as means to that end. Such decisions of course make up the constant agenda of members, officers, and trustees of institutions but they occur as a sequence of events which are rarely analyzed for the relationship they bear to overall patterns of intellectual investment. Each decision about program could be made to yield its increment to the fabrication of an institutional design. Within the design as it comes into view certain elements may be frequently repeated or manifest a prominence that will allow them to function as provisional guideposts to decision. Neither conventional academic disciplines nor simple notions of cognitive rationality are adequate guides to the structure of knowledge. Much experiment and many initiatives by single institutions are needed.

The design may be communicated to members of the university community for their consideration and response. It enters their consciousness and works its own subtle influence on their conception of their intellectual goals and their role within the institution. The design construct is not imposed by authority. Instead it is derived from the past and present characteristics of members of the institution. Trends and patterns of commitment may arise in the university rather as neighborhoods or lively centers of civic life come into existence within a city, partly by accident, partly by design. But if their character is perceived as the first outlines become apparent their development can be nurtured thereafter and brought into harmony with other parts of an emerging whole.

*The university's second objective is to develop and conduct academic programs appropriate to the different social uses of knowledge.*

The students who criticize the conventional liberal arts curriculum for its lack of relevance commonly profess a commitment to the regeneration of society. They hope to be outfitted with skills appropriate to the refashioning of institutions and social processes. What they require for this purpose is not formula knowledge of the sort found in recipe books and technical manuals (although many of them touchingly suppose that faculty members could provide such knowledge if only they could get down to doing so). What they require is knowledge of human nature, cultural history, economics, social change, politics, communications, literature, technologies, and the arts. The university already offers much that is germane to the distinctive social aspirations of this vitally important segment of collegiate youth, a fraction which is perhaps on the order of one-fourth of the whole, but one destined to play a vital role in offsetting the sorry failures of our shabby century. The tragedy is that neither students nor faculty have convincingly demonstrated that technology, the humanities, and the social sciences may contribute to the regeneration of society. By the end of this decade about half of the effort of universities should be committed to this vast enterprise, which will involve the undoing of complex allegiances to an economic system where it has been discredited by distributive injustice, greed, and ecological abandon. Painful adjustments will be required on the part of faculty, trustees, and administrators, but most of all from the public at large.

Knowledge is the principal ornament of civilization, deserving of cultivation in its own right. The university is the principal institution devoted to pure knowledge, and some appropriate part of its effort must be given to pure research, appreciation of the intellect's legacies, and training those who will pursue careers in the advancement or codification of knowledge. Indeed, such service to knowledge is perhaps a higher privilege than is generally recognized within our institutions of learning. The university as an institution has contributed to the trivialization of scholarship and to overenlistment of persons incompetent to conduct research in an attempt to create a vastly enlarged academic establishment which now faces a painful period of adjustment and reorientation. Those incapable of meeting more critical standards in research or responding to changing directions of student interest had best develop ways of protecting their income, which of course many are doing.

It seems certain that the traditional settings of professional education and graduate education, with undergraduate education oriented toward one, the other, or nothing in particular, have outlived their appropriateness. What will take their place is a major challenge to academic policy in coming years and there is not room here for conjecture about directions of change. Suffice it to say that the process of internal realignment in our institutions of learning should be guided by conscious policies informed by scholarly insight into the various functions of knowledge in society.

The university is a microcosm within which changing professional values will be tested, theories of knowledge will contend, and new methods of measurement and analysis will be developed. The policies to govern this process will be drawn in large measure from the province of social thought—from Marx and Dewey and Veblen to Marcuse and Habermas. The questions are those to which scholars in the humanities such as Erwin Panofsky and F.R. Leavis have addressed themselves, and upon which scientists such as René Dubos and Alvin Weinberg have written to good effect. Consequently it becomes possible for the first time in the history of our institutions to regard academic policy as a suitable calling for scholars, appropriate to discourse among themselves and susceptible of reinforcement from their other work. A corollary is that the practice of institutional research, developed until now as a dependency of administration, should function as a bridge between the administrative and academic aspects of institutions. If the statistics gathered in the name of institutional research do not pertain to the policy needs of the institution their collection should be discontinued. Statistical programs, like all other aspects of institutional research, should be subject to academic evaluation, review, and participation.

The search for understanding of the social consequences of academic programs has become one of the most challenging tasks facing the organized intelligence of the university. Recently the Commission on Undergraduate Education at New York University recommended an organizational innovation that seems capable of assisting in this task, an Office of Academic Research to be headed by a Director of Academic Development, to be concerned with undergraduate education, although that does not seem to be a necessary limitation. "This office should combine the functions of an office of institutional research with a broader mandate to keep abreast of developments in higher education here and elsewhere. It should develop the statistical and evaluative material that can provide the basis for continuing appraisal of the University's academic condition, as well as strategies for innovation in the University."[11] Other functions recommended for this office were to produce and circulate a series of reports on significant teaching and program developments at the university, conduct a series of seminars on processes and procedures whereby administrators should assist faculty members in their educational tasks, supervise student internships in university affairs, and develop certain university-wide committees. Such an office could be a focal point of interest regarding academic policy and offer counsel to schools and departments on the analysis of their decisions in terms suitable for use throughout the institution, in an attempt to formulate, over some years, elements of institutional design.

Working with groups of students, faculty, administrators, trustees and other community representatives, the office would observe and seek perspective on leadership, resource allocation, environmental responses, and dialogue over purpose—four untapped sources of policy sketched in the second part of this paper. In this way a foundation could gradually be laid, upon which there could rise a structure of policy adequate to formulate and serve distinctive institutional objectives.

## NOTES

1. Walter P. Metzger, "Academic Freedom in Delocalized Academic Institutions," in Metzger et al., *Dimensions of Academic Freedom* (08005) (University of Illinois Press, 1969), pp.1-33. On colleges in dispersion as open problem-solving networks see Leonard J. Duhl, "The University and Service to the Community (04004) *EXPERIMENT INNOVATION: New Directions in Education at the University of California,* Vol.3 (1970), pp.67-78.

2. Clark Kerr, *The Uses of the University* (04005) (Harvard University Press, 1963), p.8.

3. Special Committee on Sponsored Research, *Report to the Council of the Princeton Community* (25005) (1971), pp.81-86. For an analysis of the pattern of sponsored research at Berkeley, concluding that it "bespeaks a lack of coherence and central definition of purpose within the university with regard to research," see Frederick Betz and Carlos Kruytbosch, "Sponsored Research and University Budgets: A Case Study in American University Government" (07005) *Minerva,* Vol.8 (1970), p.497.

4. Charles B. Spaulding and Henry A. Turner, "Political Orientation and Field of Specialization among College Professors" (08007), *Sociology of Education,* Vol.18 (1968), pp.247-262.

5. Jerry G. Gaff and Robert C. Wilson, "Faculty Cultures and Interdisciplinary Studies" (08006) *Journal of Higher Education,* Vol.42 (1971), pp.186-201.

6. Quoted from "Rules and Procedures of the Faculty of Princeton University" by J. Douglas Brown, *The Liberal University: An Institutional Analysis* (21023) (N.Y.: McGraw-Hill, 1969), p.183.

7. Robert Hutchins, *Freedom, Education and the Fund: Essays and Addresses 1946-1956* (N.Y.: Meridian Books, 1956), pp.167-196.

8. Clark Kerr, *The Uses of the University,* p.34.

9. The University Committee on Governance, Harvard University, *Harvard and Money A Memorandum on Issues and Choices* (E02138) (November, 1970), p.8. Also Frederick Betz, Carlos Kruytbosch, and David Stimson, "Funds, Fragmentation, and the Separation of Functions in the State University" (07009), *Social Science Information,* Vol.8, no.1 (1970), pp.131-148.

10. Quoted by James A. Perkins, *The University in Transition* (21022) (Princeton University Press, 1966), pp.3-4. He suggests that institutional integrity could be achieved through "an insistence that all of the university's activities advance its capabilities to pursue each of its missions." (p.49).

11. *The Report of the Commission on Undergraduate Education, New York University* (E10003) (13 May 1971), p.6. I wish to acknowledge the advice and assistance of Dr. Louis H. Mayo, Vice President for Advanced Policy Studies, George Washington University in the preparation of this essay.

# COLLOQUIUM:
# Extending the Foundations of Academic Policy

## Proposal:
## The Promotion of Learning as the Central Objective of the University

Thomas H. Maher

Director, Program Analysis and Evaluation

University of Kentucky, Lexington

The Office of Institutional Planning at the University of Kentucky is conducting a comparative study of faculty performance review systems. It is our contention that an issue so vital to the future of the university should not be debated in the absence of insight from successful academicians and administrators around the nation.

Currently, Kentucky measures performance in much the same manner as the majority of other colleges and universities across the nation. The concepts of teaching, research, and service provide the frameworks in which legitimate accomplishment occurs. Effective evaluation is hindered by a shortage of appropriate indicators, the rather large measure of whimsy involved in the management of contemporary higher education, and an unfortunate lack of critical reflection upon the primary goals of the university. In practice, teacher performance is measured largely by student evaluation along with the usual informal assessment by colleagues and superiors. Service remains an ambiguous concept, and research proficiency is rather strictly defined as publication in a "refereed" journal.

The debate which has been generated in the course of our re-evaluation mirrors elements of the national controversy over the emerging role of the university. Some believe that our present conception of academic research is outmoded. They claim that it introduces unnecessary rigidity, limits the range of roles available to university scholars and forecloses the development of new purposes for higher education. The trend toward homogeneity among institutions of higher education is to them an outgrowth of a narrow but universally applied conception of what is legitimate scholarship.

Defenders of the existing definition argue that it generates a competitive environment which insures the emergence of that small number of individuals which will produce high quality research (as it is now defined). At the same time, however, others claim that we may be wasting the valuable abilities of those who could play meaningful roles in a broader conception of scholarship.

A pivotal proposal here holds that the university might define its reason for being as simply the promotion of learning rather than teaching, research, and service. With learning as a criterion for success or failure of university ventures, it is argued that the conceptual boundaries separating our traditional notions of teaching, research, and service might disintegrate. Emphasis would shift from production toward the utilization, and especially the synthesis of knowledge. Universities might become more interested in what has been called the activation of knowledge. Perhaps reward systems and legitimate niches could be provided for synthesizers, "translators," those marginals who operate in the intellectual interstices between the disciplines, those who seek and apply the educational implications of the disciplines, and those who belong to the emerging action-oriented disciplines which consider social invention to be a form of research.

In any event, the current academic reward system (of which Kentucky fields a representative case) has been rightly or wrongly castigated for inhibiting the flowering of the contemporary university. The consummate problem, however, lies in translating this rather vague discontent into concrete suggestions and actual strategies which might then be judged on more objective grounds.

To add new dimensions to our discussion of these questions we now invite comments from those with professional interests in the specification of institutional objectives and the appraisal of performance (guided by the following issues and questions):

> Given the emerging goals of the American university (as you interpret them), might there be an expanded definition of "scholarship" or are there possible alternative academic activities which could be legitimized for faculty with diverse orientations? Are the traditional images of academic man inappropriate for the entire spectrum of colleges and universities?

> How, in the practical order might we assess, recognize, and reward these alternative forms of scholarship?

> Is there any way in which graduate education should be revamped to insure the development of individuals capable of playing these diverse roles in universities?

> In your judgment, what are the most successful university evaluative procedures of which you are aware?

As far as we know, this invitation represents a unique approach to bringing this question into sharper focus. Analysis of responses should not only provide valuable input for our own discussions, but through a later article should be of help to many beyond the University of Kentucky.

---

# Review Essay: Subordinating Management to Policy

George S. Odiorne,
*Management Decision by Objectives* (1969)

*The Chronicle of Higher Education* (01002) 29 Nov 71, offered its report of this year's annual meeting of the National Association of College and University Business Officers under the headline, "Business Officers Seeking a Larger Role in Academic Decisions." According to Harold M. Myers, vice president and treasurer of Drexel University and president of the association, "This is an era when the business officer must assume a much more aggressive role at the executive level of management." Hans H. Jenny, vice president for finance and business at the College of Wooster in Ohio, said that "the crisis is less financial than it is conceptual" and urged that tough managerial constraints be imposed on academic decision-making. William G. Bowen, president-designate of Princeton University, predicted that the business manager would become "an increasingly active participant in the process of managing educational resources, not just as the producer of financial tables." The growing capacity of accounting systems gives the financial headquarters of an institution unrivaled potential for control of activities. Cycles in financial management create a demand for decisions whether their academic implications have become clear or not. The advent of new management techniques poses a broad challenge to conventions whereby academic administrators meekly take their cues from the professoriate. Administration is concerned with routine, repetitive operations while management involves consideration of purpose and active intervention in activities. Future directions of education and research risk being dictated by small certitudes about unit costs unless financial management is subordinated to policies well grounded in concepts of institutional purpose.

The extent to which management deals with purpose and objectives sharply contrasts with the tradition whereby business officers merely carried out instructions delivered by academic authorities. An excellent recent contribution to the literature on management practice is George S. Odiorne, *Management Decision by Objectives* (07006) (Englewood Cliffs, N.J.: Prentice-Hall, 1969), xvi, 242pp., $8.95. This book was written as a manual on problem-solving and, as its title suggests, assigns central importance to specified objectives in all management efforts. The primary technique of modern management is to define problems in terms of goals to be reached, with indicators of performance that permit measurement of progress toward such goals. "The difference between what you have and what you would like to have comprises the problem." The goal set in one example was simply to maintain quality from a production line in which unexplained weaknesses had appeared in products. The deficiency was traced to its source and a correction was made. The decision to change the manufacturing process was simple, but it was taken in the context of a system in which the characteristics of the desired result were known, so that a change of inputs could be specified and put into effect with measurable results. Logic was employed to help identify the shortcoming and relate it to the desired result. The strongest recommendation of the book is that a variety of optional solutions should be specified for each problem. Each should be evaluated for its contribution relative to its cost, and one selected. Management is seen as a technique for multiplying options so that the best way may be chosen, typified in the figure below:

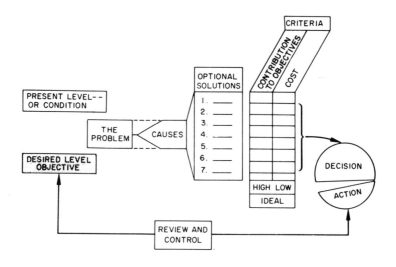

**A MODEL FOR PROBLEM SOLVING AND DECISION MAKING
BY OBJECTIVES**

The transformation of management which has occurred in recent years results from the introduction of systems concepts linking each decision to measurable consequences. Good management requires objectives to orient effort and evaluate performance and this would be especially so in the context of organizational change. Thus for an institution of learning the specification of objectives can be a way to enlist management procedures in order to strengthen its programs.

Although management is concerned with ends, most emphasis is given to the means for their attainment and it has little to offer toward defining purposes. And while "management by objectives" is widely recognized as an approach to clarifying the functions of different elements in an organization and solving problems in the course of innovation, the objectives to which the phrase refers may be the goals of a service unit or even an assignment given to a single individual. Quantitative precision is most readily attained at operating levels well below that of an institution as a whole, resulting in a tendency for management to come to focus on small units of homogeneous activity, which may ultimately complicate the task of formulating objectives overall. Management may help to implement the objectives of institutions of learning but can contribute little to formulating them. Despite their limitations techniques of management may help to organize efforts where policies have not been developed. Indeed where policies are weak or inadequate, managers may attempt to fill the vacuum with systems of their own devising—posing a threat to the delicate processes sustaining the life and integrity of institutions. In short, where our institutions are not governed by policy they may come to be managed by business officers seeking to attain greater rationality in the use of resources. In a future issue of PROMETHEUS (six) we will examine management applications of information systems technology in institutions of learning. Readers' suggestions on this topic are warmly invited, and we would especially like to know of any instances in which the operation of computerized information systems has tended to preclude professional participation in governance.

Odiorne avoids stereotyped conceptions of the management process. Mathematical procedures are impressive. He advocates their use wherever possible but cautions that they are not sufficient in the human setting, which calls for group participation in decision-making. Analysis may best be done by a single individual, but groups are usually necessary to guarantee that alternative courses of action receive fair consideration before decisions are taken. He sees the manager as an agent of organizational change whose aim is to help others achieve their objectives. He acknowledges that imponderables must play a part in decision-making and concedes that snap judgments are often required. Quoting St. Augustine on the "hidden deeps" of the human personality, Odiorne recognizes that every organization embodies values which must be preserved from management domination. He also describes mistaken efforts where analytic procedures were applied prematurely or inappropriately. *Management Decision by Objectives* is a balanced and broadly conceived book. Although written for young managers in business organizations it may be recommended as a readable treatment of management theory for officers and staff members in institutions of learning.

The use of management objectives in bureaucratic organizations is recommended in a recent article by Henry L. Tosi, Associate Professor of Management, Michigan State University; John R. Rizzo, Associate Professor of Management at Western Michigan University; and Stephen J. Carroll, Associate Professor of Management at the University of Maryland: "Setting Goals in Management by Objectives" (07007), *California Management Review,* Vol.12, no.4 (Summer 70), pp.70-78. The specification of objectives for individuals, whether by their organization or a single supervisor, is described as a threat to personal autonomy and an unproductive source of tension in a penetrating critique by Harry Levinson, president of the Levinson Institute: "Management by Whose Objectives?" (07008), *Harvard Business Review,* Vol.48, no.4 (July-Aug 70), pp.125-134. Instead of imposing tasks on staff members organizations should aid them in self-realization despite the difficulty that some people have in making their own future goals explicit. "Each of us has a built-in road map, a picture of himself at his future best. . . He can begin to spell out for himself the central thrust of his life. Reviewing all of the occupational choices he has made and the reasons for making them, he can begin to see the common threads in those choices and therefore the momentum of his personality. . . . The information serves both the man and his superior as a criterion for examining the relationship of the man's feeling and his, however dimly perceived, personal goals to organizational goals."

As Philip Abelson has remarked of the Carnegie Institution, of which he is president, the most important function of research establishments is to foster the growth of their members toward the intellectual goals they have set for themselves. The vital and reinforcing relationship between individual and institutional objectives deserves central consideration among the principles by which institutions of learning are governed. Management can either stifle scholars or widen their opportunities for professional fulfillment. It may be timely for college business officers to help their colleagues to foresee financial consequences of decisions about academic programs. But if management techniques are going to be brought to bear on academic decisions, new institutional mechanisms should be created whereby scholars and scientists may become aware of the policy implications of management approaches and protect their right to participate in decision-making.

One other dimension of management that deserves more notice than it has received from institutional leaders is preparation for management careers in institutions of learning. Vanderbilt University has created a new Graduate School of Management whose primary focus will be on training for innovation in organizations. In the words of Dean Igor Ansoff, an applied mathematician and former staff member of the RAND Corporation and Lockheed Electronics, "most schools today are turning out administrators, not effective change managers." (Quoted in "A B-School for Entrepreneurs of Change" (32001), *Business Week*, 25 April 1970).

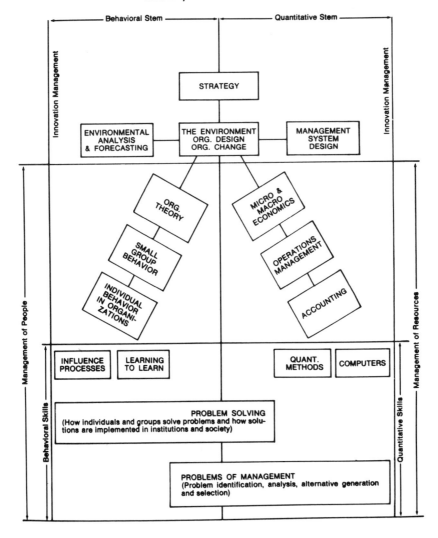

TAXONOMY OF THE CORE CURRICULUM

"The focus of the curriculum is the management of change in purposive organizations. In order to initiate change that will be effective in the pursuit of organizational and societal goals as well as cope with the change dictated by one's external environment, the manager must possess both experience and familiarity with existing practice and with a wide variety of tools for addressing the future. . . . Finally, it is becoming increasingly clear that most organizations cannot avoid interaction with organizations of other kinds. Governmental agencies affect corporations, corporations affect governmental agencies; schools affect communities, communities affect schools; foundations affect social action, social action affects foundations; and so on, thus establishing 'organizational ecology' as a proper area of concern . . . . The Masters Program addresses itself not only to the business firm, but also government hospitals and health care organizations, churches, social-action agencies, and educational institutions." From "The Masters Program," 12 pp.; also "A Strategic Plan for the Graduate School of Management, Vanderbilt University" (E37203), Sept 68, 43 pp., mimeo.

---

# Alternative Approaches to Planning and Policy in Higher Education

Robert W. McMeekin, Jr.
36 Mohegan Road
Acton, Massachusetts 01720

The commentary on the Newman Report and the response of professional associations of higher education (PROMETHEUS, One/two, July, 1971, pp. 33-5) prompt me to contribute these comments from my perspective as a participant in economic studies of higher education.

In recent discussions of the difficulties faced by higher educational institutions brought about by shrinking resources and rising costs and enrollment, three major themes have emerged: first, the need for improved planning and budgeting in the institutions themselves, in order to make better use of increasingly scarce resources; second, the need for Federal support of higher education; and third, the need to develop alternative modes of providing post-secondary education. The three themes are linked, as will be noted below. These comments attempt to place them in perspective and seek to stimulate dialogue on the subject.

Although some interesting forays in higher education planning have been made, there is still considerable resistance to application of the tools of budgetary analysis and planning in this area. A constructive scepticism is justified, because tools of quantitative analysis have severe limitations when applied in areas where "outputs" cannot be easily quantified. A major portion of the resistance, however, stems from ignorance of the methodologies involved—program budgeting, systems analysis and other tools of decision analysis—and from a gut reaction to the association between these tools and the Department of Defense.

With surprising consistency one hears comments to the effect that systems analysis got us into the debacle of Viet Nam, led to the fiascos of TFX and C5A and so on. These notes are not the proper vehicle for arguing that wrong decisions on Viet Nam stemmed from a lack of systematic policy thinking, nor for a disquisition on the uses and limitations of analytical approaches. One can only make a few assertions:

1. Systematic thinking, with attempts to clarify objectives, quantify the major variables affecting higher education and apply reasoned criteria of choice, can lead to more effective use of resources.

2. While the tools of decision analysis should be applied with judgment and circumspection, their acknowledged limitations do not impugn their value in clarifying thinking, identifying alternative solutions to problems, and increasing the effectiveness of educational endeavors.

3. The nature of thought on the subject of higher education is, with some notable exceptions, bound by the wisdom of the past, constrained by existing institutional patterns, and based upon outmoded assumptions.

4. It is ironic that, of all our institutions, it is institutions of knowledge that have so little knowledge of themselves, such vagueness as to their objectives and purpose in society, such a paucity of quantitative data about their workings, and such resistance to application of available analytical techniques in a spirit of self-inquiry.

To invoke an often-used analogy: our system of higher education is like an industry producing a product the nature of which is unknown, by a process the nature of which is unknown, which is largely paid for by people who do not consume the product, and consumed by people who have no voice in what product is offered. Add to this anomalous situation the points that the "industry" is monopolistic, that the product must be "bought" as a requisite to enjoying other (largely unrelated) benefits, and that the conditions of purchase tend to create further inequities in the distribution of income and other benefits, and the prospect fairly boggles the mind. In such a situation—and the analogy has considerable validity—the need for clear thinking regarding policy choices should be clearly evident.

While there is widespread agreement regarding the need for Federal funding, there are two conflicting schools of thought on how this should be administered. The first holds that Federal support should be distributed on the basis of centrally determined formulae, based upon enrollment and perhaps weighted to account for special circumstances. The second holds that funds should be made available to institutions on the basis of their own plans and programs. All the points above support the latter (let us call it a budgetary approach) and oppose the formula approach.

Planning for development of institutions can be carried out most effectively by the individual institutions themselves. In fact, meaningful planning must be further disaggregated to the level of the individual department or school or to even lower levels of organization. At higher levels, the choices become blurred and the essential data on program content and, importantly, program performance are lost in aggregation. There is growing awareness in the field of planning that "macro" approaches are blunt instruments and that "micro" analysis of programs and projects offers greater insight for policy decisions. These points should be borne in mind in considering methods of aiding higher education.

The formula approach to Federal funding is the antithesis of applying rational thought to the development of higher education. It foments not change and development but a perpetuation of the anomalies revealed in the analogy above. It stifles the search for new and more effective solutions to the problems of higher education. Critics of the budgetary approach, and most higher education associations are among these critics, argue that it would lead to central planning of higher education. On the contrary, it would permit far greater freedom for individual institutions to plan, innovate, and experiment.

With regard to the need to seek new modes of providing higher education, our third major theme, two points should be made. One of the fundamental tenets of systems analysis and program budgeting is the need to clarify objectives and seek alternative means of accomplishing them.

Application of the tools of decision analysis, at least at levels of policy above the trivial, does not lead to "right" answers to complex problems. These approaches to thinking about policy changes produce, at best, greater understanding of the problems and the factors that affect their solution and possible alternative means of accomplishing the ends that are desired.

If non-traditional options in the area of higher education are needed, then it should be clear that one means of supplying Federal support has clear advantages over the other. The formula approach tends to reinforce the existing situation and to create institutional constraints upon variations in the existing patterns of higher education. The budgeting approach permits and encourages institutions to plan and experiment with work-study plans (which reduce on-campus enrollment), non-traditional degree programs, and other variations on the "standard" higher educational model. Such variations would encounter problems under a uniform system of formula grants. The forces tending to perpetuate existing institutional patterns are, as recent events testify, already extremely strong. A formula approach for Federal grants, based upon enrollment in existing institutions, would add to the rigidities of the present system while obviating the need to clarify objectives, seek alternatives, and generate innovative processes of teaching and learning.

The ramifications of the elliptic statements above far exceed the scope of this brief note. The need for better understanding of the uses and limitations of analytical tools, the need for experimentation and well-designed research on alternative educational means, and the crying need for quantitative data that will permit sound planning and meaningful research—these and other points need extensive elaboration. The purpose of this exercise, however, is to elicit comments, debate and proposals, in which these ideas can be treated at greater length.

# Knowledge of Financial Institutions as the Basis for National Policy on Financial Structure and Regulation

Donald P. Jacobs, Professor of Finance, Northwestern University and Almarin Phillips, Professor of Economics, University of Pennsylvania; Staff Co-Directors, President's Commission on Financial Structure and Regulation, Washington, D.C.

The President's Commission on Financial Structure and Regulation was appointed in June 1970 to recommend regulatory changes to improve the performance of the financial system. At its early meetings the Commission defined more narrowly the areas it would cover. It was decided to concentrate on regulatory and structural problems relating to six types of financial intermediaries. These are: commercial banks, savings and loan associations, mutual savings banks, credit unions, reserve life insurance companies, and private pension funds.

The scope of the work was determined by the Commission's view of the state of the financial system in 1969-1970 and the reasons which motivated the creation of the Commission. These can be classed under two sets of occurrences. The first were effects of inflation-induced movements in the level of interest rates. The second were effects of the new technologies available to financial institutions.

The drastic changes in interest rates demonstrated an inherent weakness in the operations of savings and loan associations, mutual savings banks, and some commercial banks. These institutions were purchasing a large majority of their funds under short term contracts and using them to make long term fixed price commitments. With the steeply rising rates in 1966 and again in 1969-70, they faced an income problem which would not allow them profitably to offer rates required to retain deposits. Interest rate maximums on time and savings accounts, which had been imposed on commercial banks by the Banking Act of 1933, were extended to savings and loan associations in 1966 and prevented large scale problems of failures and disintermediation from developing. Deposit rate regulation served the dual purpose of isolating the deposit markets from the other money markets and, with an allowed differential between thrift institutions and commercial banks, protected the thrift institutions from the competitive strength of full service commercial banks. The regulations also lessened the policy loan problems of life insurance companies.

It soon became clear that the influence on deposit flow exercised by these regulations has a very short half life in periods of high market rates. By 1969-70, depositors and borrowers were learning to go around the regulated depository institutions and get higher yields or better lending accommodations. Utilization of these regulations during future periods of rising interest rates will not afford the same protection to thrift institutions.

If thrift institutions were threatened with widespread failures, it is inconceivable that government aid would not be forthcoming. Such aid could be vindicated because of size of the institutions—they have more than $250 billion of deposits—and the repercussion of failures on other deposit institutions and on the government-backed insurance funds. Another rationalization for government support would argue the industry should be aided because of its role as an instrument of public policy. It has been required to specialize in mortgage lending in furtherance of the high social priority goal of providing the nation an adequate stock of housing.

Even if deposit rate maximums could be expected to offer protection to thrift institutions in future periods of rising rates and a negatively sloping term structure, the high costs of their side effects argue against continued use. Small depositors are discriminated against. Large businesses receive a disproportionate share of available credit. Large credit flows direct to ultimate borrowers create a potential for costly liquidity crises.

The regulation of deposit rate maximums preserved the integrity of the thrift institutions but did not provide a flow of new deposits. This caused a major contraction in funds available for financing housing. Congressional targets on housing construction were not met, leading to a number of new programs of federal financing aids to housing. In 1970, these programs accounted for approximately 50 percent of new funds in mortgage financing.

The second set of problems are less directly visible than the effects of deposit rate regulations but could in the long run have a larger influence on the structure of the financial system. The technologies utilized by financial institutions determine the structure which will develop and, ultimately, the appropriate regulatory constraints. The operations of deposit intermediaries require large capability in information gathering and retrieval. Recent innovations, particularly computer-based technology, have greatly expanded the ability of financial firms to collect, analyze and retrieve information. This has increased both the geographic area and the range of products which an institution can service.

These developments have greatly lessened the impact of branching restrictions on banking structure and led to widespread movements into new product offerings. They are reflected in the recent development of the one bank holding company form of organization, itself a manifestation of attempts to circumvent existing regulatory constraints.

The financial system consists of a group of interrelated industries which compete in some product areas and also compete with non-financial firms in the provision of other services. As the discussion above suggests, the interrelated nature of financial intermediaries and the use of deposit rate maximums caused serious problems to surface in other parts of the system. This same sort of problem develops when proposed regulatory change is considered in the Congress. Consideration is required not only of the impact which will be produced on the industry directly affected, but also of the direct and indirect impacts on other financial and non-financial firms. Invariably, the granting of enlarged operating powers to one type of institution affects the position of other institutions and elicits lobbying efforts to defeat or modify the legislation.

A commission can view the entire financial system, making a set of recommendations which take account of both direct and indirect effects. In this case, a balanced package of recommendations was developed to improve performance through greater competition, eliminating varieties of anticompetitive, protectionist regulations which have historically prevailed and which are no longer needed to preserve the soundness of the system. The position of the consumer of financial services would be improved through greater competition.

The experience with monetary Commissions suggests that a set of recommendations which is well designed can be influential in guiding legislation. This is the third officially empowered monetary Commission organized in the United States. The first in the 1860's gave rise to the National Banking System. The second in the 1910's recommended the establishment of the Federal Reserve System. We ought to mention the fact, of course, that the most recent commission-type view of the financial system, the Commission on Money and Credit, had very little impact. But it should be remembered that this Commission was not officially sanctioned but was the outgrowth of the cooperative effort of two very influential private organizations, the Committee on Economic Development and The Ford Foundation.

It is our belief that the Commission on Financial Structure and Regulation has benefited from the existence of the Commission on Money and Credit, especially from the impetus that was given to research on the operations of financial intermediaries. The CFSR did not attempt to mount the broad research program which distinguished the CMC. Rather it organized its resources to take advantage of the research effort that had been made by academics, research departments of regulatory bodies, trade associations, and others. A program for Commission discussions of problems was first developed. Then a wide search was made of the literature to determine the state of research knowledge about these problems. Pertinent articles were reproduced and summarized for Commission members. Regulatory agencies and trade associations were asked to con-

contribute research and position papers in areas of their expertise. Finally, a number of academics were requested to prepare papers in areas where they had demonstrated competence.

---

# Proposal:
# A Census of Education
# and Learning

Michael Marien
Educational Policy Research Center
Syracuse University Research Corporation

"The statutory functions of the Office of Education are to collect such statistics and facts as shall show the condition and progress of education, to diffuse such information as shall aid the people of the United States in the establishment and main-tenance of efficient school systems, and otherwise to promote the cause of education."

*U.S. Government Organization Manual, 1971/72*

This paper argues that a "Census of Education and Learning" is increasingly necessary and desirable as a source of essential information for educational policy-making in an increasingly knowledge-based society. Such a "Census" would not necessarily involve a single comprehensive enumeration, but could involve an assembly of data from many sources with original data added as necessary. The Census might be conducted by the USOE National Center for Educational Statistics, the Bureau of the Census, some other new or existing public agency, or some private or quasi-private research organization. The method of compilation and the auspices of the compiler are questions to be considered after establishing the need for such a census and describing its possible scope—the only concerns that are pursued in this paper.

As a society becomes increasingly complex, there is a growing need for the systematic collection of information on its vital components. The availability of this information is necessary, although hardly sufficient, to the creation of viable public policies. The quinquennial Census of Manufactures is representative of the specialized information needs of the receding industrial era, where manufacturing activity was the dominant sector of the economy.

The major—if not central—importance of education and learning to the viability of our future society would suggest that an extensive effort be made to collect all information that is relevant to this increasingly critical policy area. But the present scope of relevant information is far too narrow to deal with the changing context of "education." By utilizing unquestioned 19th-century definitions of "education," inadequate information is brought to bear in policy-making, resulting in sterile—if not dangerous—decisions. The traditional definitions of education assume that it takes place in schools and colleges. See for example, Israel Scheffler, *The Language of Education,* (Springfield, Ill.: Charles C. Thomas, 1960). This assumption is so embedded in our society that schools and colleges are often referred to as education, therefore precluding any possibility for the process of education to occur outside of schools and colleges. As applied to individuals, a common figure of speech is that one "gets an education" or "is educated" by virtue of attending a school or college and acquiring a diploma for completion of institutional requirements. This widely accepted institutional definition, rather than any content definition of education, invites critical re-examination.

Rather than a "designated institution" definition, the alternative is simply to recognize a variety of institutions that aid learning in various degrees and in various manners. Applying this alternative definition to individuals, education is simply the total sum of what one knows, regardless of where, how, or when the learning takes place. When we refer to a "truly educated person"—one who is knowledgeable in many areas—we are employing this "sum of learning" definition. In a knowledge society, this alternative definition is far more appropriate. As actual learning grows in importance, we can no longer afford the misrepresentation of what people know and how their knowledge has been acquired. Indeed, in a purportedly scientific era, it is ironic that this fundamental confusion has escaped notice.

The designated institution definition still survives intact in the statutory functions of the U.S. Office of Education as cited at the outset of this paper. The scope of "education" is limited to "school systems" (which, today, include colleges and universities). Consequently "to collect such statistics and facts as shall show the condition and progress of education" results in collecting data on schools and colleges, which at best reflect the condition and progress of these institutions and at worst have little to say about their status. (It is not the primary function of this paper to question whether data collection satisfies the stated purposes of USOE, but to point out that the purposes are far too constricting for effective policy-making in a knowledge society.) Finally, it follows that, in "otherwise promoting the cause of education," the USOE serves to promote schools and colleges. In other words, the U.S. Office of Education would be far more accurately designated as the U.S. Office of Schools and Colleges.

## Which Comes First: New Policy on Data or New Policy Requiring Data?

A new definition of education could result from an explicit policy decision to collect a broader array of data, or from some other policy decision that consequently requires more data. The dilemma is that new information cannot be collected without some new purpose, but a basically different purpose cannot be designated without information to justify it. The basic educational policy for a knowledge society will simply be that *anyone, at any age, who can learn independently should be encouraged to do so.* This new policy will be necessary because our unprecedented learning needs are outstripping the capacities of established institutions and traditional methods of stimulating learning (i.e., "instruction"). Although there is presently a surplus of certified teachers (but not necessarily of competent teachers), there are insufficient financial resources to utilize their services. Furthermore, in a society where there is every reason to expect continued change (at least over the next decade), there will be a necessity for continuing learning for everyone—in other words, the "lifelong learning" slogan of adult educators will be increasingly taken seriously. An entire society of continuing learners cannot spend all of its time in schools and colleges. Therefore, all possible means of stimulating serious learning must be utilized. Independent learning behavior is therefore necessary and desirable.

If such a policy is initiated by law or administrative fiat at a national, state, or local level, it necessarily follows that, to encourage independent and productive learning, a full array of data will be necessitated for fully understanding who learns what, when, where, and how. It is only with such data that scarce financial resources can be optimally allocated to permit maximum individual development.

If data were to be collected in anticipation of such a development, then there would be a basis for making judicious allocations of funds. But the only justification for collecting this data would be a plausible forecast of an anticipated policy decision. Such a response to forecasting has yet to take place, and the collection of data continues to lag behind emerging social realities. This is reactionary data collection as opposed to the possibility for anticipatory data collection. Data collection as a reaction to events and policies (e.g., data on urban and campus disorders in 1967 and 1969 respectively) provides little or no help (and, indeed, may be a hindrance) in suggesting events that might take place. In a complex and dynamic society, it is doubtful that viable guidance can take place with only the help of traditional methods and ideas on collecting information.

A comprehensive data collection effort might ultimately be called a Census of Learning, but because our culture still views education as institutions, the best interim title might be a "Census of Education and Learning"—a title that suggests a consideration of both institutions and learning outcomes. Such a Census would array data on all institutions that make any conscious effort to stimulate learning, learning needs and attainments of all age groups in the population, and all possible measures of learning outcomes as a result of particular institutional services.

### 1. Data on Institutional Services

All institutions with any formally organized program to enhance learning, regardless of the quality of the program, should be surveyed as fully as possible. Even schools and colleges have not been adequately surveyed. There is still a need for up-to-date data on multi-campus systems and consortium arrangements at all levels. Due to a changing composition of the personnel in education, there is a growing need for data on all persons involved in facilitating learning—including paraprofessionals, subprofessionals, and volunteers. Data could also be collected on the extent of actual utilization of new technologies. Perhaps most important, there is no on-going effort at any level of education to measure innovation—the degree to which new methods and materials generally judged to be desirable are actually used. New "space-free/time-free institutions," many of which are extensions of legitimate institutions, are rapidly emerging, requiring significant adaptation in data collection.

Other programs of non-degree credit formal education have been traditionally neglected. Yet Stanley Moses has estimated that in 1970, there were 60 million participants (on a head count basis) in this "educational periphery" of corporate and government training programs, proprietary and correspondence schools, and adult education programs sponsored by churches, unions, cultural institutions, and schools. ("Notes on the Learning Force" (20006), *Notes on the Future of Education,* Educational Policy Research Center, 1:2, 1970) There are also many organized educational experiences for children such as summer camps, dancing schools, scouting, and religious education. Inequality of opportunities to participate in these programs is just as severe if not more so than the inequities in public schooling. Indeed, these extra-school inequities surely reinforce the problems of inequity within the schools. If expenditures for all of these formal but non-credited learning experiences were to be included in the calculation of total educational expenditures (similar to the way that the cost of drugs and office visits are part of the calculation for total health expenditures), then the cost of education in our society may well be more than $100 billion annually—making education rather than the military our major societal expense.

Data should also be collected on institutions that play a prominent role in informal education:libraries, museums, zoos, the mass media, and the arts. Although data on some of these institutions are available, this data is seldom categorized under "education," but is thought of instead as "communications" or "entertainment." Obviously, not all communication and entertainment is educational, but the rigid divisions between these realms of social activity are not empirically justified.

Finally, far greater attention should be paid to the knowledge industry and the "ed biz" in particular. In 1962, Fritz Machlup published a seminal work estimating on the basis of 1958 data that the knowledge-producing occupations (broadly defined) accounted for 26.8 percent of national income. (*The Production and Distribution of Knowledge in the United States* (03005), Princeton University Press, 1962) But there has been no follow-up to this work. There is no accounting whatsoever of even the major suppliers of educational materials (many of whom are operating national networks of proprietary schools), in that this activity cross-cuts many of the established categories in the National Income and Product Accounts. The irony of the knowledge society is that we have faint knowledge at best of even the major producers of knowledge.

## 2. Data on Learning Needs and Attainments of All Age Groups

One of the major weaknesses of the National Assessment of Educational Progress is that it makes the traditional assumption that education is only for the young. Learning attainment is assessed for only four age groups: 9-year-olds, 13-year-olds, 17-year-olds, and an "adult" group in the 26-35 age range. There are severe difficulties, of course, in securing adult respondents (as pointed out by NAEP officials). However, it cannot be assumed that learning attainments of the post-35 population are at all adequate by any modern standard. Indeed, it may be found that older age groups are less well-equipped to function in our complex society than 13- and 17-year-olds. There is considerable doubt to the assumptions (if they have been consciously made) that adults are incapable of learning after age 35, or that they have acquired adequate knowledge.

But what is "adequate" knowledge? It is difficult and controversial to set standards as to the minimum knowledge and skills required by members of our society. Perhaps several blue-ribbon agencies (publicly and privately constituted) could offer their version of social and functional literacy for our contemporary as well as our future society. Despite this difficulty, it is better to offer some standard, no matter how vague, than to fall prey to the fallacy that improvements in learning from one decade to another represent "Progress." Although this is true in a limited sense, it must be recognized that, as a society grows more complex, the minimum standards for human functioning as workers, citizens, and parents also rise. Thus one could find both improvement and growing inadequacy at the same time. The National Assessment of Educational Progress, as suggested by its title, is only constituted to search for improvement.

### 3. Learning as a Result of Institutional Services

A final major category for data collection is that of relating learning attainments to particular institutions. This is difficult to do, but every attempt must nevertheless be made. In an information-rich society, it is simply not scientific to assume that the socially valued knowledge of any student is totally or even partly a result of the services of schools and colleges. Indeed, as charged by a growing wave of critics, the schools and colleges may inhibit socially valued learning. Or, in the words of one professor, "get your degree first and then get your education."

An indirect measure of learning as a result of institutional services is to develop sophisticated indicators of client satisfaction. Indeed, positive attitudes toward learning in general may become far more important in a knowledge-based society than the presence or absence of any particular piece of knowledge in the mind of the individual. Generations of students have played the testing game, cramming in facts the night before the exam, and forgetting most of them only hours after their "knowledge" has been tested. In a knowledge society, it will be increasingly important for everyone to develop capacities for and positive attitudes toward learning. Those institutions that are most effective in promoting this outcome should obviously be encouraged. Those that are least effective should be discouraged. The social benefits arising from such a criterion would pay many times over for the costs involved in applying these standards.

### Beyond a Census

In a knowledge society, where education and learning is a matter of fundamental importance, the data collected in a Census of Education and Learning should not remain in heavy volumes of charts and tables that are used mainly by statisticians. Rather, annual "State of Education and

Learning Reports" (similar to the *Economic Report of the President*) should be issued on national, state, and local levels. And, similar to the various versions of the United States Budget, there should be full, abbreviated, and popularized versions of the "Education and Learning Report" so that as many citizens as possible can be reached. In addition to data (or social indicators) on what is happening, there should also be fully annotated inventories of all books and articles that describe what the future of education might be and/or prescribe what the future of education ought to be. Ultimately, linking in with similar documents from other nations, a multi-institutional, multi-value global idea bank will emerge. The potential interaction between these two sets of documents should not be ignored. Social indicators assembled in an Education and Learning report would greatly enhance the art of forecasting possible futures and the act of advocating desirable futures. In turn, better forecasting and advocacy would create an anticipatory and self-renewing data system that would do justice to the needs of a knowledge-based-but-not-yet-knowledgeable society.

# Identifying Institutional Goals

Norman P. Uhl
Professor of Education and Psychology
North Carolina Central University
From Research Monograph Number Two
National Laboratory for Higher Education (07010)

The Administrative and Organizational Systems program of the National Laboratory for Higher Education is designed to provide institutions of higher education with an efficient method of allocating resources to achieve specified goals. One element of the program is developing an institution's ability to identify goals considered to be of prime importance by relevant on- and off-campus groups, *i.e.*, faculty, students, administrators, community, trustees, alumni, etc. Once these goals have been established, measurable objectives can then be set and strategies for obtaining them devised. By evaluating each strategy in terms of resources needed and possible outcomes, a plan of action can be determined. Since the chosen strategy is linked to a measurable objective, it will be possible to evaluate how well the plan of action attains the objective.

To support this process, certain capabilities must exist or be developed in an institution, among them:

A procedure for clarifying and generating an understanding of goals.

The ability to derive measurable objectives from these goals.

The ability to provide the information necessary for allocating human and financial resources to support the agreed-upon objectives.

The ability to use inputs from all levels in planning and decision-making, and to obtain support for these decisions.

Proper evaluation of the degree to which the objectives are attained.

A major purpose of the AOS program is to provide models by which institutions can obtain these capabilities. The AOS program also provides an information system which makes relevant data from the models readily available for decision-making. Thus a college or university employing the AOS program might expect to:

1. Develop goals that accommodate the needs of diverse constituencies and respond to conflicting societal demands.
2. Conduct systematic planning relative to the achievement of defined goals based on research, past experience, and continuous evaluation.
3. Allocate resources in a manner consistent with goals and use resources efficiently to achieve specific objectives.
4. Involve administrators at all levels in this continuing decision-making process.
5. Maintain a high degree of support among diverse constituencies in the achievement of goals and objectives.

One of the major elements of the AOS program is to enable institutions to identify their most important goals—what they are and what they should be—as they are perceived by various groups. The process of determining goals leads to improved communication among groups, more informed opinion, and ultimately to greater agreement on the priority of goals. Once this is achieved, the complexity of the remaining decision-making processes decreases significantly.

The project under discussion contributed to the development of the AOS program by providing (1) evaluation of a procedure for obtaining from different on-campus and off-campus groups their perceptions of the present goals of their institution, as well as their preferred goals, and (2) evaluation of a procedure for obtaining convergence of opinion with regard to the importance of these goals.

## Development of an Institutional Goals Inventory

As Richard Peterson stated in a "state-of-the-art" paper on institutional goals ". . . diverse colleges must be able to articulate their unique goals in ways that are meaningful to their constituencies and other supporters if they are to expect continuation of the support necessary for their survival." (*The Crisis of Purpose: Definition and Uses of Institutional Goals* (07000), ERIC Clearinghouse on Higher Education, May, 1970) Thus, in making decisions about goal priorities, it is important to consider the views of such groups as students, faculty, administrators, alumni, and trustees, as well as specific groups outside the academic community.

Certainly, personal declarations about goals for higher education are available, for example, in a recent collection edited by C. G. Dobbins and C.B.T. Lee, *Whose Goals for American Higher Education?* (21024), (Washington: American Council on Education), 1968, Philip Werdell argues for teaching and learning as the basic functions: Lyle-Spencer argues for research—"balanced" and unclassified; John Corson, for public service; Kenneth Keniston, for social criticism; and Walter Lippman, for spiritual and intellectual guidance for the nation. While these personal declarations can be helpful, an institution which desires to identify goals which are important to the groups it serves needs an efficient method for obtaining this information. Several studies have been performed recently which attempt, through the use of a questionnaire, to identify the goals of higher education institutions.

The published work of E. W. Gross and P. V. Grambsch, *University Goals and Academic Power* (07011) (Washington: American Council on Education, 1968), stands as the most significant empirical effort thus far to examine the nature of *university goals*—specifically, as they existed (in 1964) in the minds of the faculty and administrators at 68 nondenominational, Ph.D.-granting universities across the country. Gross and Grambsch used an inventory consisting of 47 goal statements, 17 of which dealth with "output" goals (preparing students, doing research, providing public service, etc.) and the remainder with "support" goals (staff retention, involving faculty in university governance, etc.). Respondents rated the goal statements, as they related to their university in terms of present and preferred importance ("is" and "should be"). Based on 51 and 40 percent return rates for faculty and administrators, respectively, it was found that the statement "protect the faculty's right to academic freedom" (a "support" goal) was ranked highest by the combined groups both as an actual and as a preferred goal. Generally differences in goal definitions between faculty and administrators were concluded to be negligible.

The Danforth Foundation conducted a study which used a shortened and revised form of the Gross and Grambsch inventory. It was administered to a sample of administrators, faculty, and students at 14 private, liberal arts colleges. This study was designed to assist these institutions in identifying their goals and, by comparing their results with those obtained by Gross and Grambsch, to determine if a difference in goals existed between universities and small private, liberal arts colleges of limited resources. Significant agreement was found among administrators, faculty, and students on most matters relating to college goals and governance in this study. The differences which existed between "is" and "should be" responses also indicated that the three groups shared common views on the direction many of the desired changes should take (Danforth *News and Notes,* November, 1969).

In another study, a group from the Bureau of Applied Social Research at Columbia University sent a form containing 64 goal statements to the academic dean of each college in the country. The deans indicated the extent to which their colleges emphasized each goal. In general, the results demonstrated that different types of institutions had different goals, although certain goal statements were "strongly emphasized" universally, *e.g.,* "To improve the quality of instruction," and "to increase the number of books in the library." By applying factor analysis to the list of goals, relationship patterns emerged. Five broad "goal structures" (factors) were identified: orientation toward research and instruction, orientation toward instrumental training, orientation toward social development of students, democratic orientation (participatory campus governance), and orientation toward development of resources. Since this study was designed only for academic deans, the goals which it identifies may not represent well the goals of other important on-campus and off-campus groups. (S.D. Sieber *et al., A Taxonomy of Higher Education* (21025), N.Y.:Bureau of Applied Social Research, Columbia University, March, 1968)

Analysis of college goals was one aspect of a recently completed Project on Student Development conducted by and at 13 of the member colleges of the Council for Advancement of Small Colleges. All faculty members and administrators ranked 25 stated characteristics of graduates (*e.g.,* "competent in both oral and written communication," "guided by God's will") in terms of "importance for the graduates of your institution." On the basis of these beliefs, the project staff was able to divide the 13 colleges into four categories: Christ-Centered, Intellectual-Social,

Personal-Social, and Professional-Vocational. (Arthur W. Chickering, "College Experience and Student Development" (41024), Paper for the 1970 meetings, American Association for the Advancement of Science)

While the above instruments were designed to assess an institution's goals as seen by different groups, each instrument was developed for a specific type of institution (*e.g.,* universities) and/or specific types of respondents (*e.g.,* administrators or faculty). Still lacking was a single instrument which would identify the most important goals for colleges or universities as seen by both on- and off-campus groups. Educational Testing Service had been conducting various studies and literature reviews during the 18 months previous to the proposal of this study in preparation for the construction of such an instrument. This project provided the impetus needed for ETS to develop a preliminary version of an Institutional Goals Inventory, based upon a review of empirical studies, statements by activists and minority groups, and key "personal declarations" about purposes in higher education. Also, recent statements of higher education goals by boards of higher education, inter-university groups, and social philosophers were studied in an attempt to cover societal goals that institutions might well aspire to, even though not seeking them presently. Using this information, the Task Force identified 18 goal areas: *intellectual development of the student, personal development of the student, vocational preparation, religious orientation, training of graduate and professional students, research, local and regional service, national and international service, social criticism, freedom, innovation, governance, self-study and planning, egalitarianism, esprit and quality of life, concern for projecting good image, financial soundness,* and *nonacademic activities.* Several items were written to represent each goal area. For each goal statement, the respondent checked the degree of importance for the institution on a five point scale ("of extremely high importance," "of high importance," "of medium importance," " of low importance," "of no importance"). All groups responded to the goal statements both in terms of perceived existing goals and goal preferences ("is" and "should be").

## The Delphi Technique

The Delphi technique is a procedure originally developed by the RAND Corporation for obtaining a greater consensus among experts about urgent defense problems without face-to-face discussion. Of course, face-to-face discussion is the usual procedure for combining individual opinions. However, for some time it has been known that there are serious problems associated with this mode of communication. Some of them are:

1. Group opinion is highly influenced by dominant individuals who

usually talk the most, yet there is very little correlation between pressure of speech and knowledge.

2. Much discussion in group situations, while appearing to be problem-oriented, is irrelevant or biasing because it is usually more concerned with individual and group interests rather than with problem-solving.

3. Group pressure to conform can distort individual judgment.

The objective of the Delphi technique is to obtain a consensus of opinions without bringing individuals together in a face-to-face meeting; this is achieved by having them complete a series of questionnaires interspersed with controlled opinion feedback. Not only can this mode of controlled interaction among the respondents mean a savings in time and money, but it permits independent thought on the part of the participants and is helpful to them in the gradual formation of a considered opinion. It has the added advantage of providing them with anonymity. This is in contrast to direct confrontation as in a faculty meeting, for instance, which often results in the hasty formulation of preconceived notions, an inclination to close one's mind to novel ideas, a tendency to defend a previously taken stand or to be influenced by persuasively stated opinions of others.

The general procedure for the Delphi technique is as follows: (1) the participants are asked to list their opinions on a specific topic, such as scientific predictions or recommended activities; (2) the participants are then asked to evaluate the total list by a criterion, such as importance, chance of success, etc.; (3) each participant receives the list and a summary of responses to the items and, if in the minority, is asked to revise his opinion or indicate his reason for remaining in the minority; and (4) each participant again receives the list, an updated summary, minority opinions, and a final chance to revise his opinions.

A number of studies employing the Delphi technique have been performed by the RAND Corporation. One example was its use in conducting an extensive survey on predicted long-range developments, some as far as 50 years into the future, in such areas as scientific breakthroughs, population growth, automation, space progress, probability and prevention of war, and future weapons systems. A summary of responses from each round of questionnaires was fed back to the respondents before they replied to each succeeding round of questionnaires. Of interest were the contents of the predictions themselves, the bases on which respondents claimed their predictions were made, the spread of experts' views, the consistent convergence of views following data feedback, and the experts' critiques of one another's views.

Another study using the Delphi technique was conducted at U.C.L.A. in 1965. This was concerned not with long-range predictions but with developments in the near future, so that the accuracy of the predictions could be verified. In this study, 20 students were asked to forecast 16 business indexes, such as gross national product, defense expenditures, etc., using the Delphi technique. Another 20 students simply filled out questionnaires on the same topic. Of the two groups, the Delphi students' predictions were more accurate for 14 of the items, the non-Delphi group did better on two items, and in one case both groups made the same prediction. Thus the Delphi technique was not only successful in obtaining a consensus on many items, and at least a majority opinion and clearly defined minority opinion on others, but also improved the accuracy of these opinions.

Five institutions were selected for our study, including public and private, colleges and universities, large and small, predominantly white vs. predominantly black. One thousand questionnaires were sent to students, faculty, administrators, trustees, alumni, parents, and leaders of community groups, asking them to check the degree of importance of each goal as it was and as it should be. A month later the list was sent to those who had responded, with majority opinions circled in red. Those persisting in the choice of minority opinions were asked to give reasons, which were distributed to all respondents, who then made their final choice. A profile was prepared for each institution showing present and preferred importance of goal areas. That for a private, senior, coeducational, predominantly white, church-related liberal arts college, with an enrollment of 1,600 is shown below:

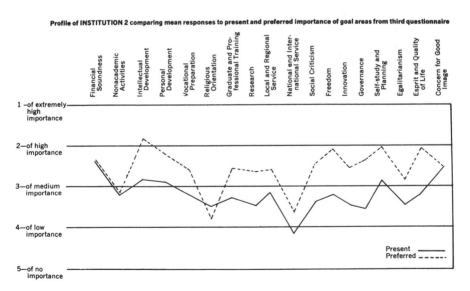

Profile of INSTITUTION 2 comparing mean responses to present and preferred importance of goal areas from third questionnaire

While there were several purposes for the study, two main objectives of this monograph were to report (1) how well the preliminary form of the Institutional Goals Inventory identifies an institution's goals as perceived by different groups, and (2) whether the Delphi technique produces opinion convergence among different on-campus and off-campus groups with regard to an institution's goals.

An unusually high percentage of participants (75 percent) completed the three questionnaires. It is highly unlikely that this excellent participation would have been possible if the participants did not view the instrument as adequately measuring their perceptions and values.

Very few goal statements were modified or additional goal statements added, even though space was provided for this purpose.

Independent of the results of this study, five specialists in higher education who had some familiarity with the institutions participating in this study, were asked to select the institutions that they thought would attach the greatest and the least present importance to each goal area. By comparing these ratings with the mean ratings of the participants at each institution, it was found that 24 of the 27 selections by those independent raters were verified by the data from the inventory.

The instrumentation and technique used in this study to assess the present and preferred goals of five colleges and universities with quite different characteristics were successful. The degree to which the instrument and the technique worked together is well demonstrated by the excellent participation achieved. Not only was the importance of goals assessed, but in most goal areas where some differences in opinion existed, agreement was achieved. This is not meant to imply that *attitudes* were changed; they may or may not have been. Possible changes in opinion occurred because participants were given an opportunity, through feedback, to consider dimensions of problems which they had not previously considered. For whatever reason, the different groups came to much greater agreement as to what the present goals of the institution are and what they should be

The Assembly on University Goals and Governance has asserted (*A First Report* (03004), Jan 71), "One thing is clear. If the colleges and universities are to improve themselves, they need to become more self-conscious about themselves, more understanding of what they have been and better informed about what is happening to them, and what their strengths and weaknesses are."

The present study investigates the suitability of combining a goals instrument and the Delphi technique to assist higher educational institutions in achieving a better understanding of their goals as seen by different on- and off-campus groups. By using this procedure, an institution not only finds out what these varied groups agree are its goals at present, but also can ascertain in what directions they agree that the institution should be heading.

The administrative technique suggested by this study offers an alternative that permits continuing evaluation to be intrinsic in institutional planning. The IGI and the Delphi technique can assist institutions in identifying those goal areas with a large discrepancy between present and preferred importance. These differences can be viewed as an indication of the degree of satisfaction with the present importance given to each goal area. Then from these goal areas, selected because of their large discrepancy, those highest in preferred importance can be identified. The areas that meet these two criteria have the greatest potential for causing dissatisfaction, tension, and even conflict. By examining the data from each group, the group or groups possessing this potential can be identified. By examining the ratings of the individual goal statements which comprise each goal area, greater insight into the nature of the dissatisfaction may be obtained.

Using the IGI as part of the Delphi technique may also be of value in other ways. For example, it is possible for the president of an institution to learn a great deal about the goal opinions of different groups. Not only can he learn what the majority believes to be important goals, but he can also become aware of minority beliefs and the reasons for them as well. Although the individual respondents remain anonymous, each group can be coded so that the college or university president can identify those groups that strongly support a goal and those who do not, with an explanation for the minority opinions. This would not only be useful to the president, but it would provide each group with a better understanding of the perceptions and values of other groups. It also offers a way for a new, high-level administrator to become quickly familiar with the perceptions and thinking of the different groups with which he will be working. In a short period of time he can obtain insight into the interrelationships of groups within his institution by reviewing the results of several administrations of the questionnaire. Instead of taking several weeks or months feeling his way, a profile of each group in terms of goals is immediately available to him. In these critieal times for higher education, academic communities are being called upon to rethink their fundamental orientations. It is important that they develop rational processes through which their constituent groups can achieve some agreement on the institution's goals.

# The Role of the Academic Planning Officer in Innovation

Allen P. Splete
Vice President for Academic Planning
St. Lawrence University
Canton, New York

University administrators are continually challenged by problems of deciding which new ideas they should nurture and implement. They are instrumental in determining what monies shall be spent and where, and how revenue shall be obtained. Administrators have the responsibility of developing effective ways of bringing all the resources of the university to bear on the innovative process within it. They have to decide, individually or collectively, which areas of interest should be emphasized to promote institutional and academic objectives.

This paper reflects my experience as a participant-observer in the innovation decision-making process at Syracuse University and the roles played by a vice president for academic affairs in the stages of this process. This experience is more fully set forth in a doctoral dissertation available upon request from the author.

By modifying definitions of stages of innovation decision making used by Everett Rogers (cf. "The Communication of Innovations in a Complex Institution" (10003), *Educational Record,* Vol. 49 (Winter, 1968), pp. 67-77.) it was possible to construct a theoretical framework within which to explore and review roles of an academic planning officer in stages of both the collective and individual decision-making process. These revised stages were: knowledge-stimulation; interest-initiation; attitude change-legitimation; individual or collective decision; and implementation.

In order to examine the academic planning officer's role in these stages, the formal correspondence and records (inter-office memoranda, letters, selected university minutes, reports, committee and project plans) of the office were screened to identify innovations with which that office was concerned over a one-year period. The seventy-two innovations thus isolated were then classified: (1) by disposition (adopted, rejected, in process); (2) source of entry into the university (external or internal); and

(3) source through which the officer learned of the innovation (external or internal). Ten innovations were selected for case study.

## The Stages of Innovation

### Knowledge-Stimulation Stage

In the knowledge-stimulation stage the officer became aware of the existence of a specific innovation and sensitive to its potential value. It appears from the research that the officer was, by virtue of his position and duties, continually a target for potentially innovative knowledge and stimulation. As such, he was sensitive to possible sources of new ideas and ready to consider current innovations for his institution. The mass media provided a veritable barrage of information. Personal contacts with alumni, other college administrators, other institutions of higher education, accrediting bodies, and other persons were additional sources of information. Legislation of federal and state governments, information about foundation and government grants available, problem situations on campus, and the emergence and confluence of his own ideas were other potential sources of innovation.

### Interest-Initiation Stage

The officer moved from the stage of knowledge-stimulation to interest-initiation when he saw potential value in an idea and was moved to seek more information about it and introduced it to others to gauge its merit. Research indicated that this officer was the actual source of entry for ten innovations in the year studied. Research indicated that the officer nurtured and promoted ideas by formal speeches, campus or local newspaper articles, attendance at college or school faculty meetings and conferences, through memoranda and letters, or personal, informal consultations with groups or individuals. Not all such communication led to new programs or novel ways of doing things, but the seeds of consideration were sown. His role might be classified as that of a "cultivator of receptiveness" as he developed a favorable climate for growth of innovations. Movement of ideas for consideration within the university is at the heart of the interest-initiation stage. When response was negative at this stage, due to lack of interest, institutional readiness, finance or other reasons, the officer suspended his activity for the time being. When response was positive, he proceeded to the third stage.

### Attitude Change-Legitimation Stage

After cultivating a receptive climate for a new idea, the officer then found himself in a position of making specific plans regarding the actual acceptance and implementation of an innovation. In this stage, the merits of the idea had to be subordinated to practical considerations of feasibility such as finance, staff, and space. His job was that of assessing the impact of proposed innovations for the university by raising pertinent questions in terms of totality of university commitment.

The officer's approval or disapproval took the form of modifying innovations, making his views known by advising faculty on proposals, expressing his thoughts on cost and staffing involved, or by allowing innovations to lie fallow in his office. The extent to which he was involved in modifying innovations was dependent on how much knowledge he possessed about them and in what stage they reached his office. If he learned that a proposal had already been forwarded to a foundation there was no opportunity for alteration. When a proposal reached him in the formulation or draft stage, however, he suggested revisions in content, other possible sources of financial assistance, or forwarded the proposal to others in the university where added interest might exist and past experience might best be drawn upon. Legitimation was a sanctioning process. Characteristic of his role in this stage was the outlining of courses of action for advancing innovations and processing them through the formal steps that marked the transition from the innovation on paper to the innovation as reality.

### Collective or Individual Decision Stage

The climate of the situation and nature of the innovation determined whether a collective or individual decision would be made and what the characteristics of the academic planning officer's role would be.

Innovations dealing with curriculum change and administrative procedures affecting faculty were decided collectively in the university senate. Responsibilities assigned to the officer determined his relationship to collective decisions about such innovations. If the innovation required university senate approval, he played some of his roles within the policy-making mechanism associated with that body, generally in senate committees or as a voting member.

Senate committees were instrumental in developing innovations for consideration by the university senate. They determined which innovations requiring action reached that body and in what form. The senate agenda committee, of which he was a member, possessed the responsibility for placing innovative proposals before the senate. By virtue of his position in the university, the academic planning officer is a major legitimizer within this committee.

When the innovation under discussion did not involve approval by the university senate and a decision on it was the individual responsibility of the officer, he worked directly with the chancellor, other vice presidents, deans, directors, faculty and staff. Individual decisions were marked by both formal and informal consultation, especially on financial considerations. The circumstances of the case determined whether the officer had discretion to adopt or reject the innovation independently, or whether advice from others was binding. The need for consultation and concurrence appeared niminal or non-existent when funds were available in the university budget for implementation or when costs were judged so prohibitive that further action at the time could not be contemplated.

### The Implementation Stage

The academic planning officer did not ordinarily participate directly in this final stage of the innovation decision-making process. When he did so it was to facilitate the efforts of others within the university in carrying out new processes.

### Summary

The role of the vice president for academic affairs in collective decisions was educational-nurturance oriented, whereas in individual decisions it was more related to policy and financial control. He was more likely to be an initiator, legitimizer and decision-maker than to stimulate or implement decision making. His role as a legitimizer due to pervasive ex-officio membership on committees was greater than indicated by previous studies of innovation decision-making in universities.

### Implications

1.  Faculty participation in collective decision-making may be greater than many faculty members realize. Collective decisions of the university senate and senate committees should be made more visible to all members of the academic community to emphasize their importance in the decision-making.

2.  An integral part of the innovation diffusion process in a university is the educational dialogue which constantly takes place among all constituencies of the university. Innovations are nurtured and decided on the basis of such communication. From such communication, administrators learn of weaknesses in existing decision-making procedures aimed toward innovation. In return, university administrators inform sponsors of innovations of sources of funding and outline procedures for gaining

adoption of innovations. This implies that the communication process in such decision-making is a learning experience for all constituencies and should be further studied as such.

3.     Much has been said about the external origin of change and innovation in a university. Relatively little discussion has taken place on how innovations enter the university and are introduced to university administrators for consideration. The findings suggest that most innovations enter the university and reach the university administrators through constituents of the academic community, particularly deans and faculty. If such is the case, more time should be spent studying relationships of trustees, administrators, deans, faculty, staff and students to the innovation process in the university.

4.     This study revealed little effort to implement innovations through use of allocated budget funds in the form of replacements for existing programs. Are faculty aware that they could implement new ideas by shifting dollars they have rather than attempting to start new programs with outside funds? Perhaps a university committed to the need for change should adopt the policy of budgeting a contingency item for emergency innovation. The reliance of private institutions on outside funds to support many innovations makes these alternatives worth careful study by sponsors of innovation.

# User Requirements: Analytic Techniques for Academic Architecture

Davis, Brody & Associates
New York, New York

The decision to expand the Science Complex at Binghamton by an approximate 600,000 to 1,000,000 square feet initiated this study by presenting a series of problems to be resolved. These related to the demands of growth and change in research and research facilities, the specific needs and conditions at the Binghamton Campus and the decision structure involved in the realization of all State University buildings.

Unpredictability and rapid change are the hallmarks of progress in all areas of scientific research, and these in turn place great demands on facilities—often resulting in the obsolescence of once modern but unadaptable buildings.

It is therefore necessary to better understand the nature of the changes taking place in scientific research and their consequent demands. In general, these changes, especially in university-based research, fall into three categories.

The most profound and unpredictable changes are those resulting from shifts in policy, planning and programming. Therefore the most important factor in how well the physical plant fits or will continue to fit the needs of the users is dependent on the managerial and educational policies set by various department heads, the division chairman, and the university administration. In the case of conflicting trends in policy, planning, or programming, the choice will ultimately fall to an individual and endure for the period of his tenure. It thus becomes essential that all decisions be made with full knowledge that not only all information from the current faculty and staff but the program itself deals with specific "first users" and that future users must be anticipated from the outset.

In addition to the effects of policy, planning and programming, changes also result less arbitrarily but just as frequently with shifts in the fields of research. In fact, it is often such changes that precipitate policy changes and dictate such major reorientations as the alliance of departments which previously worked completely independently. Although such changes are hard to anticipate and therefore difficult to plan for directly, their occurrence is frequent enough to provide a strong argument in favor of universal spaces—spaces amenable to but not tailored to the needs of any specific discipline or branch of research.

The third type of change which is constant and frequently predictable at all research facilities is due to equipment changes. Not only is new equipment for both research purposes and environmental control constantly being developed, but within any one research space the need for such equipment is always changing. This places a highly dynamic demand on all building systems from utility and services distribution to corridor widths, floor loading and laboratory sizes, all of which must be fully flexible in the ideal solution.

In addition to these factors influencing all research centers, there are at Binghamton other factors posing serious obstacles to expansion, especially on the scale desired.

Existing buildings within the Science Complex were designed when anticipated growth was far less than is now essential. As a result of initial siting in keeping with a smaller university center, the existing buildings were situated so as to define eventual limits of the site, and future expansion was intended to complete the desired interconnection of all facilities to create a true complex. Yet desired expansion now exceeds provisions within the original plan.

In addition to existing buildings, natural features and other conditions of the site and original plan pose difficulties. The academic facilities (of which the science complex forms the western portion) are bounded by an access road which provides strong definition but tight constraints on the eventual growth of the complex. Beyond this road in close proximity to the existing facilities, is planned a large number of non-science buildings including additional gymnasium facilities, a parking structure, additions to the power plant and a dormitory cluster.

To the east of the complex exists a large court central to the campus and affording a view of the distant mountains to the north. Although the grade drops off considerably in this direction, building on this slope would considerably alter the original intent of the Master Plan.

And finally, since the proposed expansion would definitely complete development within the site, it was the responsibility of this site study to see that the complex was ultimately unified and operational both as an entity and as part of the entire university center.

The problems of science facilities in general and those of the Binghamton Campus in particular present one aspect of the total problem. It is also necessary to consider the operations and procedures established to resolve these problems.

Structured to handle a large and increasing number of University Centers through all phases of planning and construction, the State University has necessarily created a wide distribution of responsibility for decision making. In the case of detailed site planning, this structure must accommodate and resolve all conflicts arising between policy, budget, master plan, program writing, scheduling, construction, etc. Ultimately, these decisions reflect or involve the people of the state, their representatives, university policy makers, site planners, architects, engineers, students, faculty, university administrators, maintenance people, etc.

In addition to a wide distribution of decision makers, there is the distant relationship between the actual users and the policy makers. Although it must be assumed that there exist certain fundamental policy agreements and overall objectives common to all parties, realizing these in concrete instances such as specific buildings is a difficult and complex undertaking.

The above outlines what this report identifies as the Problem Structure, a diagram of which is included. In brief, this diagram is an organization of the problem as follows:

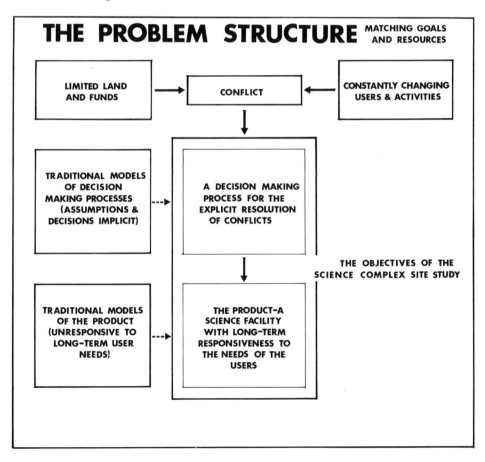

The problem to be solved exists as a result of a conflict between *needs* and *resources*. Yet the needs lack definition and the situation is compounded—especially in the case of research facilities—in that the needs, even the users and activities themselves, are constantly changing.

On the other hand the resources of the University system, in response to state policy and the like are necessarily limited. Funds must be apportioned and applied to specific problems as established by policy decisions. Also, the limits of the site and constraints of existing buildings become a prime resource consideration.

In response to the conflict between needs and resources there must necessarily be developed both a *process* and a *product*. These were the objectives of this study.

Bearing on these, however, are traditional models of the process which do not provide adequate means of presenting inherent conflicts. As a result, decisions are often made based on implicit assumptions which, could they be presented explicitly for closer consideration, might be seen in a different relation to solutions. For instance, the decision to design buildings in response to programs formulated chiefly in terms of square foot allotments instead of in terms of activities and operational procedures has a marked effect on the long-range responsiveness of facilities.

The product, too, is developed under the influence of existing models. Yet in many cases even the most accepted solution at any one time often has inadequacies guaranteeing its less than adequate performance in operation. Vertically stacked spaces have many drawbacks for use as science facilities which become apparent when the building is seen as more than just a collection of spaces; yet towers are at present a frequent response to programs for research facilities.

Organized as outlined, the Problem Structure is seen to have four aspects—resources, needs, process and product—the response to each of which is essential for solution to the actual problem.

## The Problem Solving Structure

Identification of needs and the ability to develop and consider viable alternatives is essential to problem solving.

Traditionally in the planning and design of buildings, this process is recognized and structured by the writing of the program and the architect's development and choice of a solution. Beyond this, little formal recognition is given to the myriad of interrelated steps involved in the resolution of the problem. As a result, there is little provision for either the objective evaluation of alternatives or the direct participation of all involved parties in considering alternatives or resolving conflicts as they inevitably arise.

Maintaining such an unstructured process in the interest of those aspects of design that are necessarily intuitive has been at the expense of many advantages that could be obtained from acknowledging definite steps involved in the process as both identifiable and relating directly to certain other steps.

The commonly recognized stages of design—from preliminaries and schematics on through working documents and construction—do not help to clarify the actual process of relating needs to proposals, except in a loosely chronological sense. These stages do not serve to describe the process itself.

There are, however, definite steps both essential to the design process and identifiable, and recognition of them can be extremely helpful in structuring the solution to any design problem.

The following six steps establish such a structure:

*Identification*—specifying the goals, needs, resources and priorities within the scope of the problem.

*Formulation*—generating alternative proposals, strategies and procedures for the form, content and process.

*Prediction*—stating likely consequences of alternatives based upon both rigorous and intuitive analysis.

*Selection*—finding the alternative which best meets the requirements identified in the first step.

*Management*— using the available resources of money, time and skills to effect the alternative selected.

*Evaluation*—examining consequences of the action taken and feeding back corrections for future use.

These steps identify operations implicit in any design and realization process, but without specifying a chronological order. Although certain steps proceed more easily when others are nearly complete, this structure serves more an organizational function than a scheduling one. Understanding the structure of the whole provides a framework for the organization of material and recognition of the necessary operations without implying or requiring a strict linear development. In fact, this is the actual process involved in most design problems, but since it is not acknowledged many unnecessary conflicts arise.

For example, identification of needs usually begins before formulation of alternatives; yet to expect all needs to be identified prior to formulation or to fail to see that specific formulations might imply needs other than those previously identified is to frustrate responsive design. The two steps are accurately neither consecutive nor concurrent—but they are distinguishable. Prediction and selection provide steps for recognizing and resolving points of overlap or conflict.

Application of these steps in problem solving depends largely on the scale of the operation under consideration. Hence, the Science Complex

Site Study, which at one scale involved all of the steps mentioned, might, when considered at another, larger scale, be seen as only one step—for instance, as one formulation of the alternatives open to the State University at this point in its development.

1. The misconception that the design process proceeds strictly linearly is acknowledged; individual steps are best revised or reconstructed at desirable points during the process.
2. A framework is provided for the inevitable introduction of new material.
3. The display of conflicts is invited by allowing for the presentation of various types of information and decisions in such a way that consequences and relationships must be made explicit.
4. The participation of all concerned parties is invited by organizing all information that is relevant and making selections in full view of conflicts and consequences.

Organization of these steps into a coherent framework serves more than merely those performing the operation. It provides a means by which the entire operation can be described to all involved without having to depend on premature design decisions as a measure of progress. As an alternative, progress is indicated by refinement and sophistication within each of the steps. and selection can be made with clearer understanding of consequences.

Rather than constantly converging on premature and restricting solutions, identifying the steps involved allows for continual divergence into alternatives and criteria.

This has many advantages over the traditional understanding of the process, and these advantages have considerable bearing on projects (such as the Site Study) involving a wide range of users, diverse needs and necessarily large organizations for the solution of problems.

The resources were identified by the State University in writing the contract, establishing the budget, schedules, program provisions, and site limitations. Further resources were established by selection of the Architect and his selection of staff and consultants.

To organize the resources into a useful framework, a list of variables and constraints was formulated. This list included:

Main Building Variables
      analysis of program space types
      frequency distribution of space types
      mechanical systems
      circulation systems
      structural systems

| Main Site Variables | Constraints |
|---|---|
| height | time |
| ground coverage | budget |
| phasing | program stipulations |
| boundaries | existing conditions |
| utility distribution | |
| pedestrian circulation | |

Because of the high number of variables, existing facilities both at Binghamton and other universities were used as an indication as to what variables have the greatest bearing on unresponsive solutions.

These variables were then given priority of consideration. Where existing models provided adequately responsive solutions, assumptions were made acknowledging these particular solutions as additional constraints. For example, planning of laboratory spaces is a design variable yet experience proves that grouping these provides important economies in mechanical distribution. Hence, later development of infrastructure prototypes excluded many conceivable configurations because of prior assumptions made with respect to mechanical, circulation, structure, and known flexibilities in existing conditions. As the study progressed isolation and definition of these factors came into sharper focus.

### Needs

The choice of the best formulation of the resources or the priorities necessary for their organization could not proceed from consideration of resources alone. A similar and concurrent application of the problem solving steps was undertaken with respect to needs.

Since needs are the direct result of users and their activities, the first step in an adequate compilation of requirements is the identification of users and activities. In this study it quickly became apparent that there are many ways to classify the users of the university science facilities—student, faculty, undergraduate, graduate, science or humanity student, staff, maintenance, library personnel, etc. The problem was to group these significantly and avoid undesired overlaps. The user categories selected had to not only classify all users but classify them in categories both adequately descriptive and exclusive enough to prompt statements that might be depended upon to have bearing on physical design responses.

From a detailed breakdown of users, the following list of Significant User Categories was decided upon as most useful.:

A. All Users—this category contains all users of the Science facilities and site.

B. Student/Faculty—that group of users defined by the University as members of either the student body or the faculty.

C. Instructors—those student/faculty users assuming the role of teacher whether student or faculty.

D. Learners—those student/faculty users assuming the role of student whether student or faculty.

E. Experimentors—those student/faculty users working in labs whether student or faculty.

F. Supporting Personnel—that group of users responsible for supervisory, clerical, maintenance or various support tasks.

G. Administrative Personnel—those supporting personnel doing office and/or clerical work either for University offices or student/faculty.

H. Library Personnel—those supporting personnel responsible for library materials.

I. Maintenance/Service Personnel—those supporting personnel responsible for maintaining grounds/facilities/equipment, making alterations, delivering goods, distributing materials, etc.

J. Other—all other users, including visitors, handicapped, etc.

A similar process was followed to determine Significant Activity Categories. In order to guarantee a comprehensive list of user requirements that would have bearing on the physical design it was necessary to determine what activities would be taking place within the site and proposed facilities. With these, however, the problem of overlap was far greater, and it was necessary to establish at what level of specificity to describe activities—research experimentation is certainly a different and far more discernable activity than thought or relaxation, yet they are not mutually exclusive.

While it was important not to unnecessarily limit the range of activity categories to a point where it only included the most obvious activities, the more subtle activities—certainly more fundamental, such as creativity, innovation, fruitful exchange of ideas, etc.—seemed to go far beyond implications for direct architectural response and to indicate response outside the sphere of this study. In keeping with the initial scope of the study, as limited by the existing educational and planning requirements of the State University, it was decided to describe activities in only those terms suggested by the stated program objectives for the Science Complex.

From a detailed breakdown of activities, the following list of Significant Activity Categories was decided upon as most useful:

1. All Activities—this category contains all activities taking place within the science facilities and site.

2. Circulation/Control—the movement of pedestrians and vehicles and control of such movement.
3. Experimentation/Instruction/Study—research and educational activities including both teaching and learning.
4. Rest/Relaxation—those activities not directly related to research and education or otherwise occupying programmed time.
5. Maintenance/Supervision—those activities related to cleaning facilities/grounds/equipment, making alterations, supervising grounds, attending animals, etc.
6. Administration/Clerical—those activities or faculty and staff related to programming of university or division activities as well as typing, filing and mailing in support of such activities.
7. Parking—private vehicular parking.

Having a comprehensive identification of both users and activities provided the vocabulary for formulation of a tentative list of requirement statements phrased solely in terms of the categories decided upon. These statements, establishing desired relationships between users and activities, were uniformly constructed on the model:Someone (a user or group of users) should be able to do something (an activity or group of activities) in such and such a manner (the relationship sought).

Not all requirements established in this manner had equal value, however. In addition it was realized that the value of any one statement was, in many cases, highly disputed. This was desirable since it indicated conflicts otherwise only implied, but it required a mechanism for resolution.

Therefore, a four point system of weighting requirements was adopted and each statement was evaluated according to its priority of importance on a scale ranging from zero (indicating that it was either irrelevant or unimportant) to three (indicating that meeting the requirement was essential). After a sizeable list of requirements had been drawn up from research talks with the faculty at Binghamton, experience, intuition, etc., and weighted by the architects, it was sent to the Chairman of the Science Division at Binghamton for evaluation by heads of the various departments. The list remained highly fluid and went through frequent adjustments in statement priority as well as modifications and addition of requirements.

## Process

As stated in the introduction, this report is a presentation of the process used in the formulation and evaluation of alternatives and, therefore, a description of the process would be, at this point, somewhat redundant. More accurately, however, the Site Study was not one process but several, and among them the User Requirement Method was the most significant. The development of this approach and the rationale for its application can be described in terms of the Problem Solving Structure.

As stated in the contract for the Science Complex Site Study, the objectives of the investigation were:

1. To investigate and establish criteria compatible with the educational and planning requirements of the State University and the Fund, to serve as a basis for:
2. The establishment of realistic and flexible patterns that could accommodate all of the additional facilities that will be needed in the Science Complex to fulfill its educational program in a way that will avoid serious conflict when the ultimate facilities are added to the complex;
and:
3. The development, at a master plan level, of the Science Complex including not only the proposed Biology-Psychology and library facilities but also expansion to 1974 and, if possible, beyond.

These three objectives were outlined in response to the realization that product and process are related and that it is, therefore, difficult to develop more responsive buildings without developing a method of measuring, stipulating and evaluating responsiveness.

The User Requirements Method was developed both to meet these objectives and to satisfy the need for generation of ways of examining, presenting and evaluating alternatives explicitly prior to decision making.

Traditionally, requirements have been generated as the product of research, intuition, training and experience, but their relationship to the design process and solutions has remained implicit and unstructured.

User Requirement Statements, by systematically indicating conditions and relationships which should be facilitated and encouraged in optimized design solutions, make the planning of the environment clearly open to the contributions of all those affected by decisions.

The User Requirement Method is intended as a means of revealing conflicts and evaluating design proposals by indicating explicitly consequences otherwise implied in alternative solutions. This method is a powerful tool if applied rigorously and thoroughly, but since, in concept, it is independent of program limits and deals directly with the users, it can lead to unexpected or even unwanted conclusions within a given context.

As a result, user and activity categories must be defined in terms applicable to the problem under consideration—for the Site Study, in terms applicable to architectural rather than policy response. It is to be hoped that, as more studies are programmed with this approach, a greater range of consequences can be accurately anticipated and accommodated and that more conflicts can be open to resolution by all means available.

## Product

User Requirements were formulated solely as means of evaluation. No effort was made to have these requirements generate the design proposals directly. Instead; the development of the proposals proceeded independently and made use of other concepts, the most important of which was the Space Type approach.

Concurrent with the identification of variables and requirements, programmatic information was compiled from analyses both of existing science models at various universities and of the program for the proposed Bio;Psych facilities at Binghamton. The first step in this analysis was a breakdown of areas by space name and comparison of the frequency distribution of these spaces in the various programs.

Traditional identification of program requirements has been submitted to architects by the clients as a listing of specific spaces described in terms of size and services needed. Superimposed on this technical description is usually an indication of some of the desirable relationships that must exist between spaces, implying certain undetailed operating procedures. These program relationships are usually stipulated by the first users and tied, especially in rapidly changing institutions, only to current policy and planning. Frequently, before new facilities are complete, policies have changed and planning characteristics are obsolete, requiring costly changes. Most often this is the result of fitting a built solution too closely to specific but not static requirements.

Attempts to circumvent these problems have produced totally modular buildings which, because of their uniformity, can easily accommodate change. This, however, is an expensive solution especially for laboratory facilities and has the added drawback of resulting in stereotyped planning disorienting to users.

A third approach is to combine the "close fit" and "modular" approaches by abstracting from the program certain space types that can be grouped in planning(either horizontally or vertically) to provide a more flexible, efficient and economical arrangement of spaces while at the same time allowing for a great degree of design freedom.

It was felt that it should be possible to compile programmtic information and analyses of basic space types and their distribution frequency by using terms compatible with user requirement statements and defining spaces in terms of activity types, rather than in the less useful terms of space name. Our area analysis is based, therefore, on functional distinctions of lab, non-lab and special which describe more useful categories of space types and consequently have more direct architectural implications than distinctions by space name. These functional categories were subsequently used to develop the four Preliminary Infrastructure Proposals.

While the infrastructures were under study, siting alternatives were directed by a compilation of restrictions drawn from investigations into existing conditions at the Binghamton Campus and from formulation of the variables and constraints presented above. In addition to program requirements, the eventual design criteria included the following restrictions that had to be acknowledged by all proposals:

1. Existing buildings
2. Existing and proposed vehicular circulation
3. Existing pedestrian circulation and eventual increases due to dormitory proposals beyond the Science Complex
4. Existing and proposed service mains
5. Access to existing site utilities and service areas during construction
6. Service and emergency vehicular access to all existing and proposed facilities
7. Master Plan accommodation of the view of the mountains to the north from the main campus quadrangle

These restrictions, in addition to program area requirements and projections for future growth, provided the basis for initial massing studies. These studies were eventually consolidated into three approaches which indicated the major alternatives available for satisfying the siting requirements:

Scheme A—low building height, maximum coverage, least dependence on or interference with existing facilities, greatest growth possibilities.
Scheme B—least envelope, maximum interconnection with existing facilities, greatest height and massing, greatest accord with master plan.

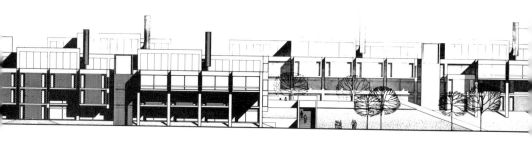

Elevation 1

Scheme C—greatest use of development to reinforce existing and proposed circulation routes, greatest import in master plan by crossing loop road.

The decision to generate these site solutions for the Science Complex by the use of an infrastructure—that is, by a system of building that is both repetitive yet spatially varied—was concluded after research in the early stages of the study. Analysis of existing science facilities had revealed that certain building types proved prototypical for nearly all science facilities in present use or development.

Analysis of existing and proposed program spaces in the Binghamton Science Complex according to the three functional variables provided the basis, however, for a complete investigation into all possible infrastructure prototypes based on these space types. Eliminating those possibilities that were not amenable to feasible circulation patterns or utility distribution or that represented mirror solutions or virtual duplication, reduced the list of prototypical infrastructures to four.

At this point, with a set of weighted requirements, a workable breakdown of space types, four infrastructure proposals and three site plan proposals, a preliminary evaluation was made to determine the advantages and disadvantages of the various proposals according to the priorities established in the user requirements.

In order to evaluate the proposals as objectively as possible, all quantifiable information was taken from drawings and recorded under the respective headings of Site Measures and Building Measures.

To reflect the varying degrees to which requirements were met, either as determined from the "measures" tabulations or deducted by the Architects, a four point scoring system similar to the weighting system was adopted. Zero indicated that the requirement had not been satisfied in the proposal under question; one indicated poor satisfaction; two, better; and three indicated that the requirement had been met fully. The product of

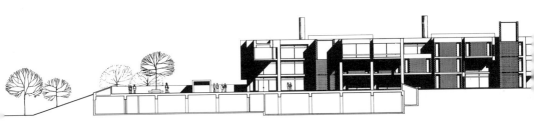

Elevation 2

this score and the weight of the respective user requirement was tabulated on a separate "Scoring Grid" for each proposal.

Prior breakdown of the requirements into the various user and activity categories provided a means of reflecting each proposal's total score in a way that revealed the implications for each user and activity category. The scoring system thus provided a user profile and an activity profile indicating the distribution within the total score and allowing for more detailed and enlightened evaluation of the proposals.

Although the results of the preliminary evaluation were by no means conclusive, the shortcomings of certain proposals became quite obvious. Of the site alternatives, Proposal B, as evaluated by the User Requirements, proved entirely inadequate in nearly every category, but the relative merits of Proposals A and C were not easily determined. Not only were the total scores virtually identical but the profile breakdowns presented similar pictures of the two proposals. As a result of this similarity it was decided that the two solutions be combined, taking the best aspects of each to produce additional proposals.

Scoring of the infrastructure alternatives produced a more marked spread indicating in part that the user requirements for the building were a sharper design tool than those for the site. Both of the taller, more compact infrastructures fared poorly in comparison to the lower infrastructures which scored highest in those categories having to do with circulation and student use. However, the infrastructure with the highest overall score, Proposal 2, failed to match the scores of Proposal 3 in either of these two categories, trading them off against advantages for administrative activities and instructors. Clearly, the direction indicated for further effort was a combination of the advantages of these two proposals and less emphasis on the taller infrastructures.

As a result of the evaluation, it was decided that the space types used to generate Area Analysis 2 were ultimately too general and fostered many design preconceptions. This led to the conclusion that space types cannot accurately be described solely as responses to activity types but could be more usefully characterized by not only activities but also by the

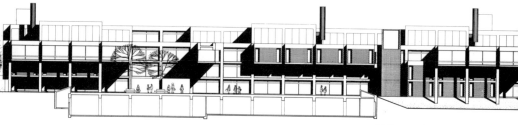

Elevation 3

number of people involved in the activities and the things required for those activities. Further, it was found that "things" had to be defined by their size, weight and system demand. In other words, a student conducting an experiment requiring piped-in service has, in many ways, more requirements in common with a janitor needing a slop sink than he does with a fellow student conducting mathematical research.

These conclusions led to discarding the previous classification of programmed and existing science spaces according to a functional (lab, non-lab and special space type) analysis and to adopting an analysis based on only two variables—bay height and mechanical-structural capacity. High and low bays with either normal or special mechanical-structural capacity produced four space types. A fifth type—other—was decided upon to include any specially shaped or unusual structure.

Definitions:

Low Bay—Spaces that are generally less than 400 sq. ft. and require a clear ceiling of 9 to 10 feet.

High Bay—Spaces that are generally more than 400 sq. ft. and require a clear ceiling of 10 to 16 feet.

Normal Structural-Mechanical—Spaces that are characterized by low demand on mechanical and structural systems.

Special Structural-Mechanical—Spaces that are characterized by high demand on mechanical and structural systems.

Other—Spaces which, due to particular activity types, extraordinary shape or loading demands set requirements that cannot be met by the above space types. These fall beyond the capacity of the infrastructure.

The Final Site Proposal, as suggested above, developed from the three site plan alternatives evaluated previously with the Site User Requirements. As a result of the scores, it was decided to concentrate on developing a combination of Proposals A and C, the schemes favoring low

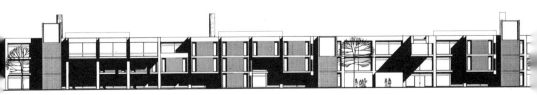

Elevation 4

buildings and extensive site coverage. The program requirements for phasing of the additional facilities posed difficult restrictions to this effort, however, and rendered many massing possibilities unworkable, but the Final Site Proposal represents the best aspects of the previous proposals as is borne out by its score against the user requirements.

### USER REQUIREMENT
### SCORING GRID
### PROPOSAL B
PROPOSAL TOTAL 139

| | | ALL ACTIVITIES | CIRCULATION/CONTROL | EXPERIMENTATION/IN-STRUCTION/STUDY | REST/RELAXATION | MAINTENANCE/SUPERVISION | ADMINISTRATION/CLERICAL | PARKING | USER PROFILE |
|---|---|---|---|---|---|---|---|---|---|
| A | ALL USERS | 16 | 45 | 2 | | | | 2 | 65 |
| B | STUDENT/FACULTY | 2 | 4 | 2 | 4 | | | | 12 |
| C | INSTRUCTORS | | | | | | | | — |
| D | LEARNERS | | | | | | | | — |
| E | EXPERIMENTORS | | | 3 | | | | | 3 |
| F | SUPPORTING PERSONNEL | | 1 | | | | | 2 | 3 |
| G | ADMINISTRATIVE | | | | | 1 | | | 1 |
| H | LIBRARY | | | | | | | | — |
| I | MAINTENANCE/SERVICE | | 42 | | | | | | 42 |
| J | OTHER | | 9 | | | | | 4 | 13 |
| • | ACTIVITY PROFILE | 18 | 104 | 4 | 5 | — | — | 8 | 139 |

### USER REQUIREMENT
### SCORING GRID
### PROPOSAL C
PROPOSAL TOTAL 194

| | | ALL ACTIVITIES | CIRCULATION/CONTROL | EXPERIMENTATION/IN-STRUCTION/STUDY | REST/RELAXATION | MAINTENANCE/SUPERVISION | ADMINISTRATION/CLERICAL | PARKING | USER PROFILE |
|---|---|---|---|---|---|---|---|---|---|
| A | ALL USERS | 16 | 76 | 4 | | | | 4 | 100 |
| B | STUDENT/FACULTY | 4 | 6 | 3 | 6 | | | | 19 |
| C | INSTRUCTORS | | | | | | | | — |
| D | LEARNERS | | | | | | | | — |
| E | EXPERIMENTORS | | | 6 | | | | | 6 |
| F | SUPPORTING PERSONNEL | | 2 | | | | | 4 | 6 |
| G | ADMINISTRATIVE | | | | | 2 | | | 2 |
| H | LIBRARY | | | | | | | | — |
| I | MAINTENANCE/SERVICE | | 48 | | | | | | 48 |
| J | OTHER | | 9 | | | | | 4 | 13 |
| • | ACTIVITY PROFILE | 20 | 147 | 7 | 8 | — | — | 12 | 194 |

**USER REQUIREMENT**

# SCORING GRID
**PROPOSAL** Final Site Plan

PROPOSAL TOTAL 287

| | | ALL ACTIVITIES | CIRCULATION/CONTROL | EXPERIMENTATION/INSTRUCTION/STUDY | REST/RELAXATION | MAINTENANCE/SUPERVISION | ADMINISTRATION/CLERICAL | PARKING | USER PROFILE |
|---|---|---|---|---|---|---|---|---|---|
| | | 1 | 2 | 3 | 4 | 5 | 6 | 7 | • |
| **A** | **ALL USERS** | 18 | 111 | 6 | | | | 10 | 145 |
| **B** | **STUDENT/FACULTY** | 6 | 9 | 3 | 6 | | | 6 | 30 |
| **C** | **INSTRUCTORS** | | | | | | | | — |
| **D** | **LEARNERS** | | | | | | | | — |
| **E** | **EXPERIMENTORS** | | 6 | | | | | 9 | 15 |
| **F** | **SUPPORTING PERSONNEL** | | 2 | | | | | 2 | 4 |
| **G** | **ADMINISTRATIVE** | | 2 | | 2 | | | | 4 |
| **H** | **LIBRARY** | | | | | | | | — |
| **I** | **MAINTENANCE/SERVICE** | | 63 | | | 8 | | | 71 |
| **J** | **OTHER** | | 9 | | | | | 9 | 18 |
| • | **ACTIVITY PROFILE** | 24 | 202 | 9 | 8 | 8 | — | 36 | 287 |

**USER REQUIREMENT**

# SCORING GRID
**PROPOSAL** Final Infrastructure

PROPOSAL TOTAL 394

| | | ALL ACTIVITIES | CIRCULATION/CONTROL | EXPERIMENTATION/INSTRUCTION/STUDY | REST/RELAXATION | MAINTENANCE/SUPERVISION | ADMINISTRATION/CLERICAL | PARKING | USER PROFILE |
|---|---|---|---|---|---|---|---|---|---|
| | | 1 | 2 | 3 | 4 | 5 | 6 | 7 | • |
| **A** | **ALL USERS** | 17 | 40 | | 6 | | 9 | | 72 |
| **B** | **STUDENT/FACULTY** | | 29 | 4 | 3 | | | | 36 |
| **C** | **INSTRUCTORS** | | 22 | 13 | | | | | 35 |
| **D** | **LEARNERS** | | 6 | 27 | 7 | | | | 40 |
| **E** | **EXPERIMENTORS** | | 12 | 106 | | | | | 118 |
| **F** | **SUPPORTING PERSONNEL** | | | | | | | | — |
| **G** | **ADMINISTRATIVE** | | 10 | | | | 11 | | 21 |
| **H** | **LIBRARY** | | | | | | | | — |
| **I** | **MAINTENANCE/SERVICE** | | 57 | 6 | | | | | 63 |
| **J** | **OTHER** | | 9 | | | | | | 9 |
| • | **ACTIVITY PROFILE** | 17 | 185 | 156 | 16 | — | 20 | — | 394 |

# Bibliography

The Refusal to Define the University—
A Characteristic American Failing.
Laurence R. Veysey, *The Emergence of the American University* 02003
(University of Chicago Press, 1965) xiv, 505 pp. $10.00, paper (1970),
$3.95. Following a period of reform that established it as a stable
institution in the 1890s, the American university gained wealth and social
status partly as a result of maintaining even among its own members a
systematic incomprehension of its purposes and allegiances, according to
this sensitive and well documented interpretation. Since then its
departmental structure and administrative routines have become fixed, as
it was in that decade that diversity of educational programs was forsaken
in the competition for growth that has continued ever since. "Few new
ideas have been advanced on the purpose of higher education since 1900,
and there have also been few deviations in its basic pattern of administration." (p.338) Differences of aim and values were concealed by a nearly
universal unwillingness to unmask a central myth, that formal education
constituted a remedy for the important problems faced by society. "As one
glances over the whole range of academic structure which had developed,
noting the disparity of the motives which cemented it from top to bottom,
it is difficult to avoid concluding that the institution would have fallen
apart had not this powerful optimistic myth captured the minds of its
middle ranks." (pp.336-37)

Our sense of novelty in the contemporary plight of the university
may not survive Veysey's account of a student commune in shacks near
Stanford that were torn down in 1902, the refusal by Harvard students of
an offer of self government in 1907, student-faculty estrangement revealed
by two nineteenth-century murders of professors by students, or the long-
standing habit of regarding students as a disployal subject population.
When faculties sought influence over the conditions of their professional
existence, sober critics deplored "revolt" in the university. Sixty years
before the specter of the multiversity the variousness of the undertakings

of the University of Chicago led it to be called "Harper's Bazaar" in a pun on the name of its first president. New rational methods of university administration were called for in the 1880s and a decade later there was a flourishing black market in themes.

The historian can find scarcely any record of reasons for decisions in the formative decade of the 1890s, because institutional leaders did not give voice to their guiding assumptions. There has been only a steady trend away from "sharp-edge thinking."

Veysey offers a penetrating insight into the vision of the men who created our major intellectual institutions, which says a great deal about their failure to formulate conscious policies: "It involves the act of seeing, stretched forth as it were on a gigantic canvas, a huge network of lines, arranged with order and precision (and yet with fascinating variety) into an aesthetically pleasing shape, like the out-of-scale maps one sometimes sees in railroad timetables. The lines here represent the invisible relations between the units of a sprawling organization. Some are darker, some fainter; some solid, some subtly dotted. To place these lines correctly and with flair requires the hand of an artist. That artist is the creative administrator." (p.369)

### Attempt to Measure Institutional Goals.

Educational Testing Service, *Institutional Goals Inventory* 07021 (Princeton, N.J.: Educational Testing Service, 1971) 13 pp. The number of institutional goal areas has been expanded to 22, with some amendment of the 18 originally tested by Norman Uhl. The list of goals statements has been expanded to 110. The instrument was tested at ten institutions in California in May in hopes of issuing a revised version for more general use in the fall of 1971. For a narrative account of the development of the revised instrument see Richard E. Peterson, "Toward Institutional Goal-Consciousness" 07022 (Berkeley, Calif.: Educational Testing Service, June 71). The following outputs are recognized in this version:

1. academic development (acquisition of knowledge, academic mastery, etc.),
2. intellectual orientation (as an attitude, style, commitment to learning, etc.),
3. individual personal development (of one's unique human potential, etc.),
4. humanism/altruism (idealism, social concern, etc.),
5. cultural/esthetic awareness (appreciation, sensitivity to the arts, etc.),
6. traditional religiousness,
7. vocational preparation,
8. advanced training (graduate, professional),
9. research,

10. meeting local needs (community public service, etc.),
11. public service (to regional, state, national, international agencies),
12. social egalitarianism (meeting educational needs of people throughout the social system),
13. social criticism/activism (toward change in American life).

All of the above are considered to be output goals and those that follow, support goals:

14. freedom (academic, personal),
15. democratic governance (emphasizing structural factors),
16. community (emphasizing attitudinal factors—morale, spirit, ethos),
17. intellectual/esthetic environment (intellectual stimulation, excitement, etc.),
18. collegiate environment (extracurricular activities, social life, athletics, etc.),
19. innovation,
20. evaluation and planning,
21. accountability/efficiency, and
22. external relations (toward understanding and mutually beneficial relations between campus and external constituencies).

### Activity Measures for the Single Institution.

Educational Testing Service, *Institutional Functioning Inventory* 09001 (Princeton, N.J.: Educational Testing Service, 1970). Available from the Institutional Research Program for Higher Education, Eldon Park, Director. A survey instrument with 72 questions for students and 60 additional questions for faculty, administrators, and others, whereby they may indicate attitudes and awareness of institutional characteristics and programs, is now offered to institutions of higher education by the Educational Testing Service. Also available, "Prospectus" 18 pp. and "Preliminary Technical Manual" vi, 63 pp.

### Origins of Institutional Functioning Inventory.

Educational Testing Service, *Conversations toward a Definition of Institutional Vitality; Background Discussions during the Development of a Measure of Vitality in American Colleges and Universities* 09002 (Princeton: Educational Testing Service, 1967, 112, xiii pp. Conference transcripts of discussions about problems of measuring the vitality of educational institutions.

### Institutional Research in the University: A Handbook

BY Paul Dressel and associates. 07018 (San Francisco: Jossey-Bass, 1971) $12.50. Large universities generally establish offices of institutional research to achieve uniformity in statistics on enrollment. The functions of such offices have been broadened to include the collection of many different kinds of data, which makes them centers for statistics on institutional activities. This handbook offers a reinterpretation of institutional research as the evaluative self-study of a college's goals, operations, and accomplishments. It advances proposals for the establishment, organization, and operation of offices of institutional research in academic institutions, on the assumption that statistical data have ready applicability to the determination of policies.

### Institutional Research, Lack of Academic Impact.

Ernest L. Boyer, *Institutional Research and the Academic Program* 07020, "New Dimensions in Higher Education" No.20 (U.S. Department of Health, Education, and Welfare, U.S. Office of Education, April 67), 76 pp. E.D.R.S. 013-381 $0.50 MF, $3.04 HC. Boyer cited three major areas of institutional research which had constructively influenced institutional management: facilities studies, cost-analyses, and enrollment studies. But he found no comparable contributions to academic program: "the curricular and instructional dimensions of higher education have remained relatively fixed." (p.20) He entered six recommendations aimed at enhancing the policy applicability of institutional research:
1. to sharpen the identity and purposes of institutional research as a profession,
2. to probe more fundamental educational problems.
3. to develop comprehensive and empirically supported theories,
4. to orient institutional research toward institutional change,
5. to disseminate findings more effectively, and
6. to become part of an institution's commitment to change.

"The immensely important activity of institutional research has failed, on the whole, to make significant contributions to the real business of education, which is to do the best possible job of transmitting knowledge, stimulating the growth of intellectual maturity, and discovering new knowledge.... What is in short supply is the wholehearted desire to seek better ways to teach, to communicate, to administer. If nature abhors a vacuum, it also resists displacement; and human nature, having had several thousand years to refine natural law, tends to resist forces that even seem to lead toward personal displacement. And so when all is said and done, the question of whether educational research is to become a vital force in academic affairs depends on the individual faculty member, dean, department head, president, addressing his own professional posture and saying, 'There may be a better way . . .' and meaning it." (pp.46-47)

### Institutional Research, Early Development.

A. J. Brumbaugh, *Research Designed to Improve Institutions of Higher*

*Learning* 07019 (Washington: American Council on Education, 1960) 56 pp. E.D.R.S. 017-141 $0.25 MF, $2.32 H.C. This important study helped to lay a foundation for expanded programs of institutional research oriented toward the policy needs of institutions of higher education. The examples given and the arguments advanced tend to indicate that the early contributions of institutional research were to functional efficiency rather than instrumental service to distinctive institutional objectives.

### Outputs of Higher Education.

Ian McNett, "Assessing College Effectiveness" 07012, *Change* (Jan.-Feb., 1971), pp.13-14. Report on the status of the Planning and Management Systems program of the Western Interstate Conference on Higher Education (WICHE), and its attempt to evolve "output indicators" for higher education.

### The Search for Identifiable Outputs of Higher Education.

Western Interstate Commission on Higher Education, *The Outputs of Higher Education:Their Identification, Measurement, and Evaluation* 07004 (July 70) vii, 130 pp. $3.50. Seminar papers and bibliography, available from WICHE, P.O. Drawer P, Boulder, Colo. 80302.

### Institutional Appraisal and the Search for Leadership.

Frederick deW. Bolman, *How College Presidents Are Chosen* 09000 (Washington, D.C.:American Council on Education, 1965), 60 pp. $1.00. Of 115 new college presidents surveyed, 48 reported no specific or detailed discussion in advance of their appointment about the formal long-range plans of the institutions over which they had been chosen to preside. Bolman strongly recommends that the search for leadership begin with a sophisticated determination of the needs of the institution, quoting one faculty member of a selection committee as follows: "The board of trustees and any selection committee should make a thorough analysis of an institution, and of the immediate goals of that institution, before undertaking to hunt for a president. I think few institutions really take the task seriously; certainly this institution didn't. But it is idiotic to build lists of names or to enumerate criteria for a president if you don't know where your institution stands, where it wants to go, and what it needs in the way of an executive head." (pp.23-24)

### Government Abhors a Policy Vacuum.

Lyman A. Glenny, Robert O. Berdahl, Ernest G. Palola, and James G. Paltridge, *Coordinating Higher Education for the '70s* 03007 (Berkeley, Calif.: Center for Research and Development in Higher Education, 1971) xiv, 96 pp. The following are among what the authors regard as minimum powers for state coordinating boards of higher education: "to engage in continuous planning, both long-range and short-range; to acquire information from all postsecondary institutions and agencies through the establishment of statewide management and data systems; to review and approve new and existing degree programs, new campuses, extension centers, departments and centers of all public institutions, and, where substantial state aid is given, of all private institutions . . ." (p.7) One function proposed in all seriousness for such boards is to analyze the state's needs for manpower while assessing requests to establish new academic programs. If the flow of students across state lines makes this hard to assess, then coordinators may turn to regional higher education boards and interstate compacts. Program review might also extend to major research grants, of (say) $200,000 and up! All of this review effort will of course be based upon comprehensive information systems, such as "the WICHE-PMS systems (which) build on the HEGIS package." (p.77) As "a consequence of better information systems and greater attention to the specific goals of program budgeting and to management-by-objective technologies" such boards may proceed to regulate "the actual outputs of education." (p.78) Freedom is, of course, just another word for nothing left to lose.

### Loss of Institutional Autonomy.
John Walsh, "California Higher Education: The Master Plan Faulted" 21030, *Science,* Vol.164 (16 May 69), pp.811-13. The advent of centralized state planning for higher education is traced to "the pathology of the present situation" in California, in which political factors are seen to loom large.

### Budgetary Chaos and Statewide Coordination.
Frederick Betz and Carlos Kruytbosch, "Sponsored Research and University Budgets: A Case Study in American University Government" 07005, *Minerva,* Vol.7 (1970), pp.492-519. A case study of the University of California that demonstrates how institutional integrity can be lost in conflicts of purpose and procedure in the support of research.

### Academic Responsibility: Freedom's Precondition.
Special Committee on Academic Freedom, Responsibility, and Tenure, American Association of State Colleges and Universities, "Statements on Academic Freedom and Responsibility and Academic Tenure" 41007, *Chronicle of Higher Education* (15 Nov 71), p.6. "Academic freedom is the right of members of the academic community freely to study, discuss, investigate, teach, conduct research, publish, or administer, as appropriate to their respective roles and responsibilities. It is the responsi-

bility of administrators to protect and assure these rights within the governing framework of the institution." The statement enumerates a number of responsibilities upon which academic freedom is considered to depend, and restricts the claims of academic freedom to teaching and research within each scholar's professional field.

### Educational Research: The Quagmire Deepens.

Roger F. Levien, *National Institute of Education: Preliminary Plan for the Proposed Institute* 41029 (Santa Monica, Calif.: RAND Corporation, (1971), Report 657-HEW, xvii, 199 pp. While confessing that the problems to be addressed by educational research are not yet determined (!), this report lays out a plan for a new education research agency with a starting budget of $130 million to grow by an additional billion over ten years. One rationale offered is that no more than one-fourth as many dollars are spent for research and development in education as in agriculture, while the two fields were comparable at 5 and 7 percent of GNP respectively. Consider this statement: "Illumination of the nature of education's crucial problems would be a major function of the NIE: the intramural R&D activity would play a central role in this process. However, that illumination has not yet been performed, so an adequate definition of problems warranting national R&D efforts does not exist." (p.viii) The proposed Institute would administer training programs and other projects devoted to "moving the state of the art forward" at all levels of education, preschool to doctoral. Three-quarters of the Institute's resources should be devoted to problem-oriented research and development and the advancement of educational practice. The remaining resources would be for the support of studies in adjacent disciplines such as psychology or educational media and for a program of intramural research. Also the text of S.434, A Bill to Establish a National Institute of Education (29 Jan 71) 8 pp.; Statement by Secretary Elliott Richardson to the Select Committee on Education of the U.S. House of Representatives (17 March 71) 8 pp.; Statement by Commissioner of Education Sidney P. Marland, Jr., to the same committee (17 March 71) 9 pp.; and Statement by Don Davies, Acting Deputy Commissioner for Development to the same committee (14 May 71) 3 pp.

### National Foundation for Higher Education.

Statement by Elliott L. Richardson, Secretary, U.S. Department of Health, Education, and Welfare, before the Subcommittee on Education, Committee on Labor and Public Welfare, U.S. Senate (4 March 71) 13 pp. and handout, 7 pp., U.S. Department of Health, Education, and Welfare (Feb 71) 41020. Plan of organization and summary of proposed legislation offered by Clark Kerr, *Change,* Vol.3, no.3 (May-June 71), p.8 ff.

**Study Commissions on Higher Education.**
Morris Norfleet and Dan Coleman, "Higher Education under the Microscope" 21029. Paper for the American Association of State Colleges and Universities. July, 1971, 11 pp. Lists directors, purpose, program, source of support, and members of eight major study groups: the Commission on Non-traditional Study, the Commission on Academic Affairs, the National Commission on the Future of State Colleges and Universities, the Carnegie Commission on Higher Education, the Newman Task Force, the Committee to Explore Exemplary Innovations in Post-Secondary Education, a Study on Restructuring Higher Education, and the Assembly on University Goals and Governance.

**Society for College and University Planning.**
Publishes a bimonthly bulletin, *News,* with occasional inserts of essays and articles. Annual subscription $10.00 in North America, $15.00 elsewhere. Proceedings of three annual conferences on campus planning available: 1966 ($2.00), 1967 ($5.00), and 1968 ($4.00); also *An Annotated Bibliography on University Planning and Development* (1969), 158 pp., $5.00 and *Campus-Community Relationships, An Annotated Bibliography* (April 71), 63 pp., devoted to geographical topics. H. Gilbert Nicol, Director, 616 West 114th Street, New York, N.Y. 10025.

**Failure of Collegial Policy-Making.**
Dwight R. Ladd, *Change in Educational Policy: Self-Studies in Selected Colleges and Universities* 07013 (N.Y.: McGraw Hill, 1970). 231 pp. $5.95. For the Carnegie Commission on Higher Education. Analysis of thirteen attempts to reformulate educational policy by consultation and consensus, conducted in the 1960s at leading institutions, led Ladd to conclude that "we have passed the limits of collegiality as an effective system of decision-making." He also described faculty resistance to recommendations for change.

**Academic Policy and Institutional Integrity.**
Stephen J. Tonsor, "Power, Authority, and University Administration" (07016), *Congressional Record,* 27 Oct 71, S16883-87. Proposes that policy-making authority be vested in university boards of trustees, aided by an investigative secretariat, and criticizes faculties for selfish attention to their personal and professional interests at the expense of institutional integrity. Entered into the *Congressional Record* by Senator James Buckley (R., N.Y.).

**Instilling Social Allegiance Seen as College Goal.**
John A. Howard, President, Rockford College; David Andrews, President,

Principia College; Alexander Jones, President, Butler University; and Roy F. Ray, President, Friends University, "Report on the Present Circumstances of Higher Education" 21019, submitted to Robert H. Finch, Counselor to the President, Oct 70. Entered in the *Congressional Record,* 4 Nov 71, E11858-861 by Congressman Marvin Esch (R., Mich.). "The promotion of attitudes of affirmation, appreciation, and commitment, to counteract a prevailing enthusiasm for criticism and dissent" is recommended as "essential to the proper functioning of all higher education in this country."

### Policy-making in the Turbulent Institution.
*Selected Bibliography on Institutional Governance and Campus Unrest* 41000 (Washington, D.C.: American Council on Education, Dec 70), 4 pp.

### Roles and Responsibilities in Governance.
Harvard University Committee on Governance, *The Organization and Functions of the Governing Boards and the President's Office; A Discussion Memorandum* E02138 (March 71) 40 pp. The memorandum affirms the trust responsibilities of governing boards on behalf of "the public which even for a private university determines its objectives." Implicit throughout the report is a finding that too much time of the Corporation, president, and financial staff is devoted to routine detail and that overall institutional planning, especially its educational dimension, has suffered as a result.

### A Prescription for Continuous Institutional Renewal.
New York University, *The Report of the Commission on Undergraduate Education* E10003 (13 May 1971) 137 pp. Recommends the creation of an Office of Academic Development to incorporate institutional research, combined with twenty student internships to support continuous study and reappraisal of the university's educational offerings.

### International Study of Education Policy.
Irving J. Spitzberg, Newsletters for the Institute of Current World Affairs, 31005, 535 Fifth Avenue, New York, N.Y. 10017, to which requests for copies may be addressed.

### The Total Learning Population and Education Policy.
Stanley Moses, *The Learning Force: A More Comprehensive Framework for Educational Policy* 20006 Occasional Paper 25, Syracuse University Publications in Continuing Education. 37 pp. $1.25 from the Library of Continuing Education, 107 Roney Lane, Syracuse, N.Y. 13210. National

education policy might extend beyond the traditional institutional "core" of schools and post-secondary institutions to include a vast "learning force" of individuals seeking educational experiences through extension, educational media, correspondence schools, churches, welfare agencies, and business, which Moses estimates to involve over 80 million participants.

### Decision-Making in the University.
Dwight R. Ladd. Paper for the National Conference on Higher Education, March, 1971. 13 pp. 07014 If all constituencies of an institution were well represented on its board, they could grant its president much more effective power than usual, and enforce accountability by oversight and review.

### Evaluation of Foundation Activities.
Stephen White. N.Y.: Alfred P. Sloan Foundation, 1970. Occasional Paper, 15 pp. 07015 On request, 630 Fifth Avenue, New York, N.Y. 10020.

### Individual Goals and Organizational Objectives;
A. *Study of Integration Mechanisms,* by Jon H. Barrett, Center for Research in the Utilization of Scientific Knowledge, Institute for Social Research, University of Michigan, R48104, 1970. ix, 119 pp. $3.00. Barrett compared the fulfillment of organizational and individual purpose through a survey of skilled and professional workers in an oil refinery, employing a quantitative index of goal integration based on answers to questions about the extent to which the company satisfied their individual needs and *vice versa.* The greatest effectiveness was found where individual and organizational goals were considered to be reinforcing rather than just compatible. Although objectives are here defined simply as the functions of organizations rather than the purposes distinguishing institutions this study encourages the belief that institutional objectives must be substantially derived from the professional aims of their members.

### Governance and the Concept of Community.
President's Commission on the Organization of the Faculty, Dartmouth College. Summary statement E03755 (6 April 71) 60 pp. Recommends creation of an overall Council with a novel scheme of voting to guarantee representation to determined minorities, as well as faculty reorganization, appointment of a dean of undergraduate studies, and creation of a program of public policy studies.

# Other Literature Cited

Categories Correspond to Classifications of Holdings
in the Archives of Institutional Change
3233 P Street, N.W., Washington, D.C. 20007

## INSTITUTIONS IN KNOWLEDGE AND PRACTICE

### Reference Works, Journals

01002 *Chronicle of Higher Education,* 65.

### Studies of Inter-Institutional Relations

03004 Assembly on University Goals and Governance, *A First Report,* 90.

03005 Fritz Machlup, *The Production and Distribution of Knowledge in the United States,* 81.

### Studies of the External Social Relations of Institutions

04004 Leonard J. Duhl, "The University and Service to the Community," note, 61.

04005 Clark Kerr, *The Uses of the University,* note, 61.

### Planning and Policy Development

07000 Richard E. Peterson, *The Crisis of Purpose: Definition and Uses of Institutional Goals,* 83.

07005 Frederick Betz and Carlos Kruytbosch, "Sponsored Research and University Budgets: A Case Study in American University Government," note, 61.

07006 George S. Odiorne, *Management Decision by Objectives,* 65-68.

07007 Henry L. Tosi, John R. Rizzo, and Stephen J. Carroll, "Setting Goals in Management by Objectives," 68.

07008 Harry Levinson, "Management by Whose Objectives?" 68.

07009 Frederick Betz, Carlos Kruytbosch, and David Stimson, "Funds, Fragmentation, and the Separation of Functions in the State University," note, 62.

07010 Norman P. Uhl, *Identifying Institutional Goals,* excerpts, 83.

07011 E.W. Gross and P.V. Grambsch, *University Goals and Academic Power,* 83.

### Human Values within Institutions

08005 Walter P. Metzger *et al., Dimensions of Academic Freedom,* note, 61.

08007   Charles B. Spaulding and Henry A. Turner, "Political Orientation and Field of Specialization among College Professors," note, 61.

## Administrative Processes and Management
09000   Fred deW. Bolman, *How College and University Presidents Are Chosen*, 50.

## Organizational Behavior
10003   Everett Rogers, "The Communication of Innovations in a Complex Institution," 92.

# SOCIAL FUNCTIONS OF INSTITUTIONS OF LEARNING

## Universal Popular Education
20006   Stanley Moses, "Notes on the Learning Force," 80.

## Higher Education
21022   André Gorz, "Destroy the University," 8.

21023   J. Douglas Brown, *The Liberal University: An Institutional Analysis*, 48-49; note, 61.

21024   C.G. Dobbins and C.B.T. Lee, *Whose Goals for American Higher Education?* 83.

21025   S.D. Sieber *et al.*, *A Taxonomy of Higher Education*, 86.

## Scientific Research
25005   Special Committee on Sponsored Research, *Report to the Council of the Princeton Community*, 45-46; note, 61.

## Improvement of Society's Use of Human Resources
32001   Business Week, "A B-School for Entrepreneurs of Change," 69.

# INSTITUTIONS BY TYPE AND LOCATION

## Educational Institutions
41009   U.S. Department of Health, Education, and Welfare, *Report on Higher Education*, 70.

41024   Arthur Chickering, "College Experience and Student Development," 87.

E10003   New York University, *The Report of the Commission on Undergraduate Education*, 60; note, 62.

E02138   Harvard University, University Committee on Governance, *Harvard and Money: A Memorandum on Issues Choices*, note, 62.

E37203   Vanderbilt University, "A Strategic Plan for the Graduate School of Management," 70.

# Index

Excluding Bibliography

Abelson, Philip, 68.
Academic planning, 92-96.
Academic research, 60.
Accountability of the university, 8.
Adams, John Quincy, 35-38
Administration, abolition of, 32; devolution to faculty, 32; distinguished from management, 65; lack of change since 1900, 114; reorientation of institutional research away from, 60.
Admission requirements, abolition of, 31.
Analytic procedures in decision-making, 65-68.
Ansoff, Igor, 69.
Assembly on University Goals and Governance, 7, 90.
Astrophysics, 37.
St. Augustine, 67.
Bell Telephone Laboratories, 56.
Betz, Frederick, note, 61; note, 62.
Bicentennial of American Revolution, 38.
Bolman, Fred deW., 50.
Bowen, William G., 65.
Brewster, Kingman, 43.
Brown, J. Douglas, note, 61.
Bureaucracy in universities, 28.
Butler, Nicholas Murray, 43.
Careers in management, 69.
Carnegie, Andrew, 13.
Carnegie Institution of Washington, 68.
Carroll, Stephen J., 68.
Caws, Peter, 7-34.
Census of education and learning, 77-83.
Centennial Exposition, 37.
Center for Research and Development in Higher Education, 47.
Change, management of, in purposive organizations, 70.
Citizenship, education for, 15; contrasted with higher learning, 36.
City, university compared to, 55.
Cognition, studies in, 40.
Columbia University, 43, 52, 86.
Commission on Money and Credit, 76.
Commitments of institutions, control of, 47.
Corson, John, 83.
Counseling, criticism of, 21; elimination from universities, 31.
Cultures within institutions of learning, 46.
Cumulative grade averages, insanity of, 22.

Curriculum, criticisms of, 20.
Danforth Foundation, 86.
Davis Brody & Associates, 97-113.
Decentralization of institutional resources, 50-51.
Delphi technique, 87-89.
Democratic theory, inapplicability to governance, 8.
Dewey, John, 60.
Dobbins, C.G., 83.
Dubos, René, 60.
Duhl, Leonard J., note, 63.
Education, affective, 17; and social uses of knowledge, 59; as unconscious social function, 29; changing relations of professional, graduate, and general, 59; higher, degeneration into training and information, 39; institutional alternatives, 77-83; secondary, breakdown of, 24; sequence, 23.
Educational Testing Service, 87, 115.
Educational theory and research, sterility of, 30; recommended topics for, 30.
Emerson, Ralph Waldo, 50.
Entrepreneurship, 44.
Environmental relations of institutions, 52-53.
Esperanto, 30.
Evaluation of teaching, 63-65.
"Every tub on its own bottom," 51.
Factions, administrative and professional, 47.
Family, university should not assume functions of, 16.
Federal Reserve System, 76.
Financial institutions, 74-77.
Formulas in federal aid to higher education, 72-73.
Gaff, Jerry, 47, 61.
Gorz, André, 8.
Governance, designing out of institutions, 32-34; faculty participation, 95; group vs. individual decision-making, 67; hierarchical model of, 43; relation to institutional goals, 79; role of leadership in, 49; role of the academic planning officer in, 92-96; subversion of by administrative conventions, 23.
Grambsch, P.V., 83.
Gross, E.W., 83.

Habermas, Jurgen, 60.
Harvard University, 50, 62.
Hegemony of academic institutions in seeking and exposing truth, 39.
Henry, Joseph, 36.
Higher learning considered the true province of the university, 26.
Hippie movement, 16-17.
History, reduced to status of myth in academic institutions, 38.
Horoscopes, rationality by comparison to university grading practices, 22.
Huntington Library, 56.
Hutchins, Robert, 49, 61.
Increase of knowledge, 36.
Information-rich society, 83.
Innovations and academic decision-making, 92.
Institutional change, characterized as drift rather than a process of purposeful choice, 46.
Institutional functions, incompatibility among, 44.
Institutional research, closer relation to academic policy recommended, 60.
Institutions, defined as purposive corporate entities, 41; dialogue over purpose, 54; ecology of, 52-53, 70; exchanges of views on goals, 83-91; financial, 74-77; innovations discouraged by pattern of federal funding, 73; lengthened shadows of individuals, 50; of knowledge, lack of self-knowledge, 71; outputs of, 115-16, 118; truth residing in, 39.
Jacobs, Donald P., 74-77.
Judgment, individual, contribution to policy, 50.
Keniston, Kenneth, 83.
Kerr, Clark, 44, 49, 61, 62.
Knowledge, academic programs appropriate to social uses of, 59; as a social utility, 56; of financial institutions, 76; ornament of civilization, 59; primary concern of the university, 16, 55-60, 63-64; pure, 57; representation of structure of, 57; social distribution of, 79-80.
Kruytbosch, Carlos, note, 61; note, 62.
Kuhn, Thomas, 45.
Langley, Samuel, 37.
Lascaux, 11.
Leavis, F.R., 60.
Levinson, Harry, 68.
Lippman, Walter, 83.
Localized academic institutions, 42.
Machlup, Fritz, 81.

Maher, Thomas H., 63-65.
Management, relations to policy and administration, 65.
Maps of knowledge as orientation aids to students, 21.
Marcuse, Herbert, 60.
Marien, Michael, 77-83.
Martin, Warren Bryan, 50.
Marx, Karl, 60.
Marxist theory of the state, 27.
Mayo, Louis H., note, 62.
McMeekin, Robert W., Jr., 70-73.
Median levels of intelligence, unlikely to benefit from university-level education, 13.
Medieval forms in academic architecture, 42.
Metzger, Walter, 42, 61.
Micawber, Mr., 46.
Minorities, admission to universities, 12.
Moses, Stanley, 80.
Multiversity, 49.
Museum research and education, 38-39.
Myers, Harold M., 65.
National Assessment of Educational Progress, 81.
National Banking System, 76.
National parks, analogy to universities, 10-12.
National Laboratory for Higher Education, 83.
New York University, 60-61.
Objectives, academic programs oriented toward social uses of knowledge, 59; consultation regarding employing Delphi technique, 83-91; distinguished from functions, 48-49; equated with goals, 7-8; failure of prospective presidents to discuss prior to appointment, 50; goal inventory, 115; management by, seen as threat to freedom, 68; *Management Decisions by Objectives*, review essay, 65-68; of the Smithsonian Institution, 36; of universities, relation to other institutions and to society, 9; proposal to redefine in terms of learning, 63-65; seen not to govern the process of management, 67; self-realization by members of institutions, contributions to, 68; statement of, for Princeton University, 48-49; university, representation of structure of knowledge as, 57; use by management in bureaucratic institutions, 68.
Objects, truth residing in, 38-40.
Odiorne, George S., 65-68.
Officers of institutions, role in policy, 43.

Orientation of students to university
  resources, 32.
Panofsky, Erwin, 60.
Pedagogy, 19.
Perkins, James A., note, 62.
Phillips, Almarin, 74-77.
Phrenological testing, 22.
Planning, architectural, 97-113.
Planning, considered as the search for
  balance in institutional functions, 57
  problems of purpose, 70-73.
problems of purpose, 70-73.
Plato, Academy, 19; *Republic*, 7.
Policy, and social thought, 60; data
  requirements, 79; defined as relation of
  institutional performance to objectives,
  41; educational, 54; erosion of, 43;
  foundations of, 55; lack of and exploitation of the poor, 54; leadership and
  individual judgment in, 49-50;
  obstacles to formulation in the educational system, 73; potential sources for,
  48; regarding environmental responses
  of institutions, 52-53; resource allocation, 51; should be guided by scholarly
  insight into social uses of knowledge, 60.
Power, sharing among constituencies, 43.
President's Commission on Financial
  Structure and Regulation, 74.
Princeton University, sponsored research
  study, 45-46; statement of objectives,
  48-49.
Problem-solving, 65-68, 97-113.
Professionalism and officialism in educa-
  tion, 39.
Protests addressed to secondary schools
  by university faculty, 31.
Propaganda, 38.
Pursuit of the unconventional by the un-
  fashionable, 40.
Remedial training, removal from univer-
  sity proper, 31.
Requirements for graduation, elimina-
  tion of, 31.
Research, Smithsonian Institution, 37.
Resource allocation, 51.
Responsibility of university faculty to ex-
  ternal social values, 8.
Revolutions, perpetuating the status quo, 9.
Ripley, S. Dillon, 35-40.
Ritterbush, Philip C., 41-62.
Rizzo, John R., 68.
Scheffler, Israel, 78.
Scholarship, trivialization of, 59.
Scrutiny of institutions, 39.
Self-sufficiency of isolated institutions, 42.
Smithson, James, 35.

Smithsonian Institution, 35-40.
Spaulding, Charles B., note, 61.
Splete, Allen P., 92-96.
Sponsored research, 45, 61.
State University of New York at Bing-
  hamton, science complex, 97-113.
*Statuere*, root of word "institution," 41.
Stimson, David, note, 62.
Students, capacity for continued learn-
  ing, 22; intellectual appetites of, 17;
  present vs. future, 12; stifling intellec-
  tual initiatives of, 20.
Symmetry of teaching and learning, 19.
Theorists of education, ineffectiveness of, 29.
Tosi, Henry L., 68.
Touster, Saul, 20.
Training centers, 17.
Trust obligations of U.S. in accepting
  Smithson bequest, 36.
Truth, revolutionary qualities of, 39.
Turner, Henry A., note, 61.
Uhl, Norman P., 83-91.
U.S. Bureau of the Census, 56, 77.
U.S. Department of Defense, 71.
U.S. Office of Education, 77-79.
Universal right to cultural and civic edu-
  cation, 14.
University, academic programs and the
  social uses of knowledge, 59; Balkani-
  zation of, 48; configuration of intellec-
  tual effort, 58; cultural mission of, 57;
  knowledge as primary mission of, 16,
  55-60, 63-65; lack of pre-eminent universities in Washington, D.C., 53;
  presidents, 50; presumed monopoly on
  truth-seeking, 39; the principal institution devoted to pure knowledge, 59;
  primary objective of, to represent the
  structure of knowledge, 57; resem-
  blance to a city rather than a monastery, 55.
University of Kentucky, 63-65.
University of the Witwatersrand, 57.
University State, 28.
University Teaching Institute, 19, 31.
User requirements analysis in academic
  architecture, 97-113.
Vanderbilt University, 69.
Veblen, Thorstein, 60.
*Washington Academic Calendar*, 53.
Washington, D.C., failure as a center of
  learning, 53.
Weather, research and monitoring, 37.
Weinberg, Alvin M., 60.
Werdell, Philip, 83.
Wilson, Robert, 47, 61.
Yale University, 43.